I0164090

Independent Publishing Of Ebooks:

How To Sell On Kindle, iTunes, Barnes & Noble, Kobo, Flipkart, Clickbank, and Your Own Ebook Store

A. William Benitez

Independent Publishing
Of Ebooks:
How To Sell On Kindle, iTunes, Barnes & Noble, Kobo, Flipkart, Clickbank, and Your Own Ebook Store

A Positive Imaging How-To Ebook

A. William Benitez

Published By

Positive Imaging, LLC
http//positive-imaging.com
bill@positive-imaging.com

No part of this publication may be reproduced in whole or in part, or stored in a retrieval system, or transmitted in any form or by any means, electronic, mechanical, printing, photocopying, recording, or otherwise without written permission from the publisher, except for the inclusion of brief quotations in a review.

Copyright   2016   A. William Benitez

ISBN 9781944071196

Contents

Notes

Introduction

There are long lists of markets for ebooks and many ways to create them. There is no one best way, so the methods described herein are the ones I use for publishing my ebooks. They aren't the only methods nor necessarily the best. However, I've used them successfully for years. As you read this ebook, you may well come up with ideas to improve upon the methods, and you are encouraged to do so.

The tools used to create the final manuscript for an ebook are the same as those used for creating a paperback book. Microsoft Word is the most common, and the one I use. There are other word processor and text creation applications that could work including OpenOffice, a free office productivity suite. Since the final manuscript is just the edited version of your book, it's only the first step in the actual creation of an ebook, the tool you use is not as important as the value of the content.

With both the Kindle and Smashwords (iTunes, Barnes & Noble Nook, Kobo, Flipkart, etc.) markets, Word, or a similar word processing software, is the application I find best to format the final manuscript for the ebook conversion process required by each market.

NOTE: If you plan to reach markets such as Clickbank or to market ebooks directly from your website, a good desktop publishing program will help you create a well-formatted ebook and an excellent pdf file for the final product. This is even more important if you plan to publish print books with companies like Createspace. The best and lowest price desktop publishing program I've used is PagePlus made by the British company Serif.

Of course, many will immediately state that publishing software is too expensive to purchase for an individual who publishes one book. That may have been true in the past but not any longer. I started using PagePlus X4 in 2007 and have created the print ready files for more than twenty four print books and over a dozen pdf ebooks. PagePlus is easy to learn and comes with a complete, built-in user guide and additional resources including many excellent templates for various projects including books. And the best part is that some versions are often available from Amazon.com for only $20.00. While there are new versions, including PagePlus X9 as I write this, they are unnecessary for creating good pdf files for books.

If you have any questions please email me at bill@positive-imaging.com .

1

Reasons for Writing an Ebook

Your reasons for writing an ebook can set the tone for the entire writing process. It probably isn't possible to list the many reasons why someone would want to write an ebook. Some write for the sheer joy of it and the potential for making money either doesn't enter into the thinking or isn't an important consideration.

Money or not, most write ebooks because they have something to say or something they would like to teach others. Some write because they wish to entertain others with good stories. Others are simply interested in telling everyone about their life or that of family members. There are no wrong reasons to write. Wanting to write should be enough for anyone.

Profit is certainly a good motive for writing an ebook. Writing is a great way to make a living, but profit may not be your motivation. If writing an ebook and publishing is your dream; then that is what you should do, and this ebook will help you get it done.

For me, writing has always been about making money. I enjoy the writing, but my goal has always been to profit from what I write. For that reason, I write about my knowledge and experiences and over the years I've managed to teach many people about various topics. In spite of the joy it gives me, I have never considered a writing project simply for the joy of it. But that's just me, and you may be completely different. That doesn't make your book any less valuable.

You may have an idea for an ebook from which you could profit. Perhaps you have a skill that others wish to learn and your ebook about it could help them to learn those skills. It may be a hobby that others would enjoy or a small business idea. If you have some basic knowledge that seems popular, what you know could make a good ebook. It could be an ebook about a specific niche. This book, for example, is in the independent publishing ebooks niche.

As with many of my ebooks, this one is based entirely on my first-hand experience. Many writers use their first hand experiences to write valuable and informative ebooks that help readers to do many things. It quite possible that you have a wealth of valuable knowledge that others would like to read about and comprise great topics for ebooks.

Only you can determine which method is best. You might even consider associating with someone who has a marketable skill and work with him or her to write an ebook about their skills and how others can learn how to do it and perhaps even make money following the instructions in the ebook.

Any combination of these methods will work. It's not unusual to see an ebook with more than one author. In these ebooks both writers bring something to the ebook and together it becomes an interesting, cohesive, and valuable ebook. Some hire ghost writers because they have all the knowledge necessary but simply lack the skills to write it down in an organized and comprehensive manner. A ghost writer can use the information to come up with an ebook that contains the individual's knowledge, and this person would take credit for the book.

The important thing is not to allow yourself to be discouraged. If you want to write and publish a book then do it now.

2

Planning The Book - The Outline

The Plan

Step one for any ebook, after the basic idea, is to create a clear and concise plan. Doing this requires setting your objective. If you just want to write with no thought of profit you can jump right to the outline stage below.

If profit is the main objective of your writing, you must establish your niche. Once you know the niche or topic of your book, find the market for that particular niche. That is, determine who will buy your ebook and where you can find these readers.

Knowing your market is critical because if you are unable to locate readers interested in your topic, it may be that a niche doesn't exist or is so small as to make reaching it difficult and unprofitable. While this ebook will not deal directly with marketing and promotion, the odds of an ebook selling are increased if you know your market and write your ebook to fulfill their needs. Since your intent is to profit from writing your ebook, this is a good time to revisit your concept and determine if you can alter it to make it more marketable or perhaps abandon the idea and look for a marketable niche.

Once you determine your reason for writing the book, start planning by creating an outline for your book.

The Outline

Start by writing down all the major topics you wish to convey to your readers. Put them all down without attempting to flesh them out or place them in order. At this early stage spending too much time on individual topics could cause you to lose focus on the main topics. After you have listed them all, organize them in the best possible order so that each topic logically follows the next.

Now flesh out each topic one at a time and add whatever thoughts come to you. There is no certain length for this and forget about structure. This is the thought development stage to cover as much as you can before starting to write. As you do this, new thoughts, topics and ideas will come to you. Don't dismiss them; write them down as they come to you even if they belong elsewhere. You can move them later. The important thing at this stage is not to lose the thought.

The Final Format

In this early planning stage, you also need to determine the final format. Kindle, iTunes, Barnes and Nobel Nook are popular, but may not work for ebooks that require a much larger page. There is a larger Kindle, but it is considerably more expensive than the standard model or the Kindle Fire which is the one to which you should aim your ebook. There are other kinds of ebooks that work perfectly well even with letter size books.

Other chapters in this ebook will cover the other ebook methods including Clickbank and your own web site.

3

Creating the First Draft

Once you have an outline that covers every topic in your ebook, determine if you need additional research, it should be fully compiled by now. If you still need more research, finish that and enter the additional information in the outline, so it's well organized before actually sitting down to write. Once you start you want it to flow with as few interruptions as possible. Questions may come up during the writing that require stopping to get answers but try to keep this to an absolute minimum.

That doesn't mean that you stop learning. As your book progresses, keep reading information of interest and maintain a notebook on everything you do relating to the topic. Ideas can appear at any time and from anyone. If new ideas on a topic arise while you are writing and they contribute to the topic, include them in the ebook.

Personal Stories

Use stories of personal experiences to help your readers develop a better understanding of specific topics or to emphasize your meaning regarding a specific point. These should be sprinkled throughout the book as they make reading more interesting, and readers usually enjoy these experiences, especially if it involves learning from a mistake. Such stories convey your humanity and get readers interested in you.

Using The Outline

Use the outline to write your book. Don't just print it out and use it as a guide. Double space after each topic and then write on that specific topic as many paragraphs as it takes. Don't worry about the formatting during the writing as this is a draft and requires only a normal style without special formatting. You should be thinking only about your topic, not about how the formatting will look best.

Don't Edit While Writing

Don't try to edit as you go along. Write down all your thoughts on a specific topic to make certain you give your readers an in-depth look at every aspect of the topic. Editing will come later, but now you want to make certain that nothing is left out. Don't concern yourself about potential redundancies. Later, during the editing, you can eliminate them or even merge them to make one clear sentence or paragraph.

Complete the entire book using this technique. It allows you to go back to each topic and read through it after reviewing the outline of that chapter. Working within the outline helps you to remember every detail you wanted to write about and keeps things relatively organized, and this will help later with the editing.

Each time you review the outline stirs new thoughts to add to the chapter. Don't limit yourself to the outline. It is intended to help guide you through every topic you want to cover but if you have an idea for a chapter that's not in your outline, put it down right away and continue writing. Then you can come back and flesh it out in full. Adding these thoughts stir even more ideas each time you do a review.

Don't hesitate to add anything that contributes to the value of the ebook. If you read a lot on your topic or perhaps blog about it, new things come to mind, and this will be even more solid information for your readers. Keep this up during the entire time you are writing your draft and it will increase the value and quality of your book.

4

The Discipline of Writing

Set Aside A Time To Write Everyday

Set aside time to write and make it every day if possible. Write as much as you can during each writing session and always try to complete each separate topic before moving on to the next. Avoid stopping in the middle of a specific topic. Finish writing out every thought while it's fresh in your mind to help the ebook flow and help you avoid forgetting information about a topic.

Once you have gone through the entire outline and have the first draft, read the entire thing while the outline listings are still in the file. During this first reading check for the chapter listings. Identify the chapter headings and the content that will appear in each chapter.

Protect Your File

Now the most important thing is to protect this file. Save the file as it is and then click **Save As** and give the file the name of the book or a part of the name and add the date. For example, for this book it could be **independentpublishing_10_19_16**. Once saved, open the new file and then carefully delete all the outline listings, so all that remains is the book content with the chapter headings and it becomes your first draft ready for editing. Now save the file again and then back it up before your begin editing.

Backup of your writing files is critically important and often overlooked with disastrous results. The single most important and most forgotten fact about data backup is that it involves two copies of the data. As simple as that sounds I find that many people use flash drives or other external drives to keep their data and simply work direct- ly from those files.

Once you have completed your first draft and removed the outline listing, you are ready to begin editing. Even at this stage you can still add to the book if you learn some new and valuable information that will contribute to the topic or help readers to get more out of the content.

5

Choosing the Best Title for Your Ebook

Choose your title carefully because it can contribute significantly to the successful marketing of your ebook. First, make certain that the title relates directly to the content of your ebook. As simple as this sounds, it is often ignored. The reader should learn exactly what your ebook is about and something about the content by simply reading the title even if it's brief. The subtitle should follow up by adding to the clarity but it shouldn't be essential and definitely not the sole explanation of the ebook content.

Keywords and The Keyword Tool

Your title should contain searchable keywords directly related to your book's niche. Searchable means keywords that are searched for regularly, especially on Google. You can start by deciding what you believe is the best keyword for the niche you have selected. In the case of this ebook they are Independent Publishing, Kindle and How-To Ebooks. Then you go to the Google Keyword Tool to find related keywords. You can find this tool at:

https://adwords.google.com/select/KeywordToolExternal

It's a simple tool to use and will give you some valuable information. The main function of this tool is to help those who use Adwords ads but you can use it to learn about the popularity of words and phrases on Google search. The first time you use it you are required to use a captha to make certain you are a person and not some robot trying to glean information automatically. A captha is the code you must copy accurately to enter various sites. After going through that you need only type in the words or phrases you want to check out. The tool will not only give you information regarding the popularity of your word or phrase but also create a long list of alternatives and their popularity. These alternatives are especially helpful in creating subtitles.

With the title of your ebook strive for a high ranking by making certain your title is searched for regularly and in reasonably large numbers. Take some time to develop a good title. Make certain it isn't too busy so as to make the text confusing or difficult to read. It should be clear at a glance and on a web site. Don't hesitate to change it several times as you progress through the writing of your ebook and the preparations for publishing. You want a cover that will give you the best potential for a sale no matter where your prospective buyer sees the ebook.

The Book Cover Font

The title of your ebook is critically important but it will be of little use online if the font is too small to view clearly. A large font is important because the first view of your ebook online will be the small cover photo. It is just barely larger than a thumbnail and a title will only be readable if it is a large enough. This is why a short title followed by a concise subtitle is so important. The title can be brief and as large as possible so it is easy to read while the subtitle is smaller but still readable especially after it is clicked on.

6

Editing Your First Draft

Hiring an Editor

Many writers believe it is essential to hire a professional editor to edit their book or ebook and this is certainly a good idea because your familiarity with the content may cause you to overlook things that could improve your ebook. However, this poses two problems that must be dealt with carefully. The first is financial, good editors are well paid so professional editing could require a significant investment. Such an investment is problematic for authors, especially if profit is not your main objective.

The second issue is your voice of the ebook. Writing an ebook is a personal thing and having someone make significant changes to it can be traumatic. For an editor to read your ebook to find and correct typos and grammatical errors and offer suggestions to improve your writing is really a help. Good editors can help increase the value of your book. However, for an editor to do major rewriting that makes the ebook sound like someone else wrote it, is a serious problem. Naturally, how good a writer you believe yourself to be and how important it is to you to maintain your voice in the book will determine the seriousness of the problem. If you going to hire an editor for your ebook, make certain he or she understands what you expect before the job is started.

Editing Your Own Ebook

You can edit the ebook yourself but it can be tricky and the final quality could be disappointing. There is a tendency to fall in love with your words and resist giving up any of them. If this can be overcome, there is a method of being your own editor that should work if you follow it carefully.

Step one is to put your draft aside for at least two weeks. Then, read it carefully filling in any additional information that may come to you as you read and editing as you go. Many new ideas will popup that will add value to your ebook and now is the time to add them. Reading your draft carefully will shed light on issues, errors, or incomplete thoughts that require more work. Don't hesitate to add anything that adds value to your content. More importantly, don't hesitate to remove duplications or verbosity. This is the time to fix any obvious errors. After you have completed this step put the draft aside for another week and then begin the next step.

Step two is to read your ebook aloud. This will help you hear awkward phrasing. While doing this, pick up obvious errors but don't try for perfection during the first read. Once you have finished put it down for one more week and then go through it slowly and carefully and edit it filling in any last minute ideas you may have.

If you are unsure about any section or paragraph in a chapter, try reading through it backwards. This sounds silly but it works because your brain is unaccustomed to the words in this fashion and misspellings and other problems will pop up.

The waiting time described previously may cause impatience or seem like a waste of time, especially if you are in a hurry to get your ebook published. It really isn't wasted time if you plan to edit your own work. If you don't put it down your mind will become accustomed to seeing certain errors and simply overlook them. So, instead of improving your draft by correcting errors you will become certain that everything is correct and ready for publishing. This is a mistake that will cause you to wind up with an ebook having many errors. Another thing that you can do once your ebook is fully organized exactly as you want it is to read the chapters out of order. Start reading from a chapter in the middle of the book and then jump around to other chapters in some random order. Change the order of the chapters each time you read through the ebook. This could open your mind to errors that it may not pick up if you read the ebook in the normal order.

A Good Editing Tool

There's no replacement for a good editor, but after all the steps previously described, you can improve your writing with online editing tools. There are many online editor companies, but my favorite is Grammarly. You can test it free to see how helpful it is to your writing by going to http://grammarly.com . It is free for use with the Chrome browser, but there is a fee to use it with Word. The best way to use it with Word is to download the Grammarly application and install it on your computer. Once installed it will work with Word whenever you enable it. It also works with Outlook. It is an excellent product that I've used for years, and it's helped improve my writing.

Grammarly points out misspelling, poor grammar, and poor word choice. It is a great tool for getting your writing in final form after you have done some serious editing. Use it every time you make changes to your content. After running through Grammarly, your ebook is ready for a final edit. If you feel qualified to do it yourself, wait at least one week before you start. If you know someone whom you respect and trust to edit your ebook, make use of them. If your budget allows, hire a professional editor. Even though it can get expensive, it will be much less because you have removed most of the mistakes.

Notes

7

Creating An Ebook Cover

The level of difficulty involved in creating your own ebook cover is directly related to your skills with graphic software and your design skills. Anyone with good skills, creativity, and software can create good covers.

There are many options for creating a nice cover for your ebook. If you intend to publish with Kindle exclusively then you can use the KDP Cover Creator. You can use this software free when you publish through Kindle Direct Publishing or KDP.

There are two covers for this book. For one I used PhotoPlus X6 is an excellent and, most importantly, inexpensive graphic software application developed and sold by Serif, the same British company that created PagePlus X4. At this writing, PhotoPlus X5 is available from Amazon.com for $19.99 but that could vary over time.

To see the steps involved in creating the cover for a book similar to this one with PhotoPlus X6 check out http://positive-imaging.com/cover where you'll find instructions and screen shots. So, for a small price you get a tool that will easily handle all your cover work and many other photo related tasks.

The second cover was created using the Createspace Cover Creator and complete instructions for using it are in my book **How To Independently Publish Print Books With No Investment** available from Amazon.

Of course, a third option, hiring an artist to create a cover for you, is always available and can be expensive. Check out the rest of this chapter for ways to do it yourself and then decide how you want to handle your own book cover.

Let's start with the KDP Cover Creator since it is the quickest and easiest way to create a cover for a Kindle ebook.

To create Kindle books you must have or create an Amazon account so you can sign into the web site. Just go to https://kdp.amazon.com and sign into your account. This will take you to the Bookshelf which will be empty unless you have previously published Kindle ebooks.

The next step is to click on the Create new title and fill in all the details of your book where it says Enter Your Book Details. On this page you can upload your ebook interior and then click on the Launch Cover Creator button as shown below.

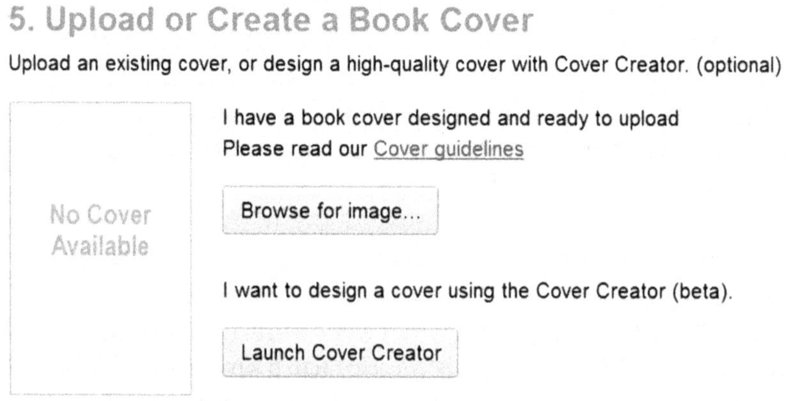

5. Upload or Create a Book Cover

Upload an existing cover, or design a high-quality cover with Cover Creator. (optional)

	I have a book cover designed and ready to upload Please read our Cover guidelines
No Cover Available	Browse for image...
	I want to design a cover using the Cover Creator (beta). Launch Cover Creator

Once you click the Launch Creator button it will go to the page called How to Use Cover Creator as shown on the next page. I have placed on the page vertically so the image is large enough to be clear and easy to read.

How to Use Cover Creator

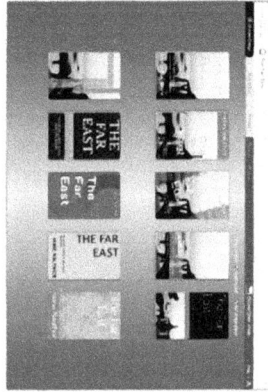

1 Choose Design

Select an initial design concept for your cover.

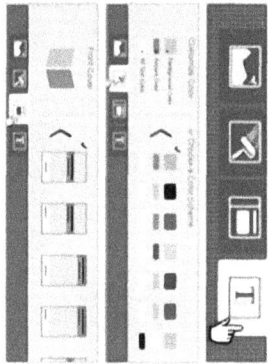

2 Style & Edit

Customize the layout of your cover by changing the position of elements, colors, and typefaces.

3 Preview

Preview your book cover before you publish.

☐ Got it. Don't show me this again.

Continue

The next page will give you three choices. Select an image from their gallery as I did, an image from your computer, or just skip this for now and move to the next step.

Get images for your cover

Select an image from our image gallery or upload one from your computer

From Image Gallery

Browse our image gallery for thousands of royalty free images.

From My Computer

Placeholder Image

Skip This Step

If you choose to use the image gallery you will have many options to categories to choose from and within each category a long list of options. Take your time and find something that fits your book.

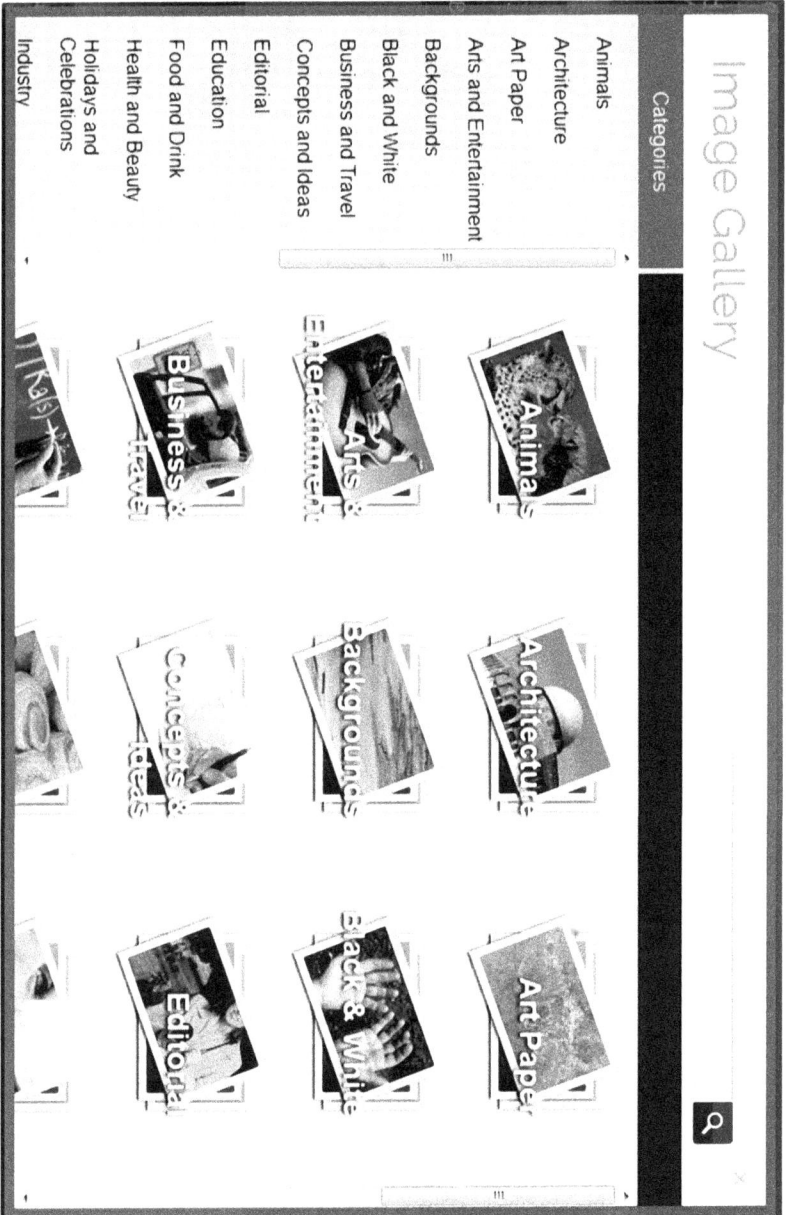

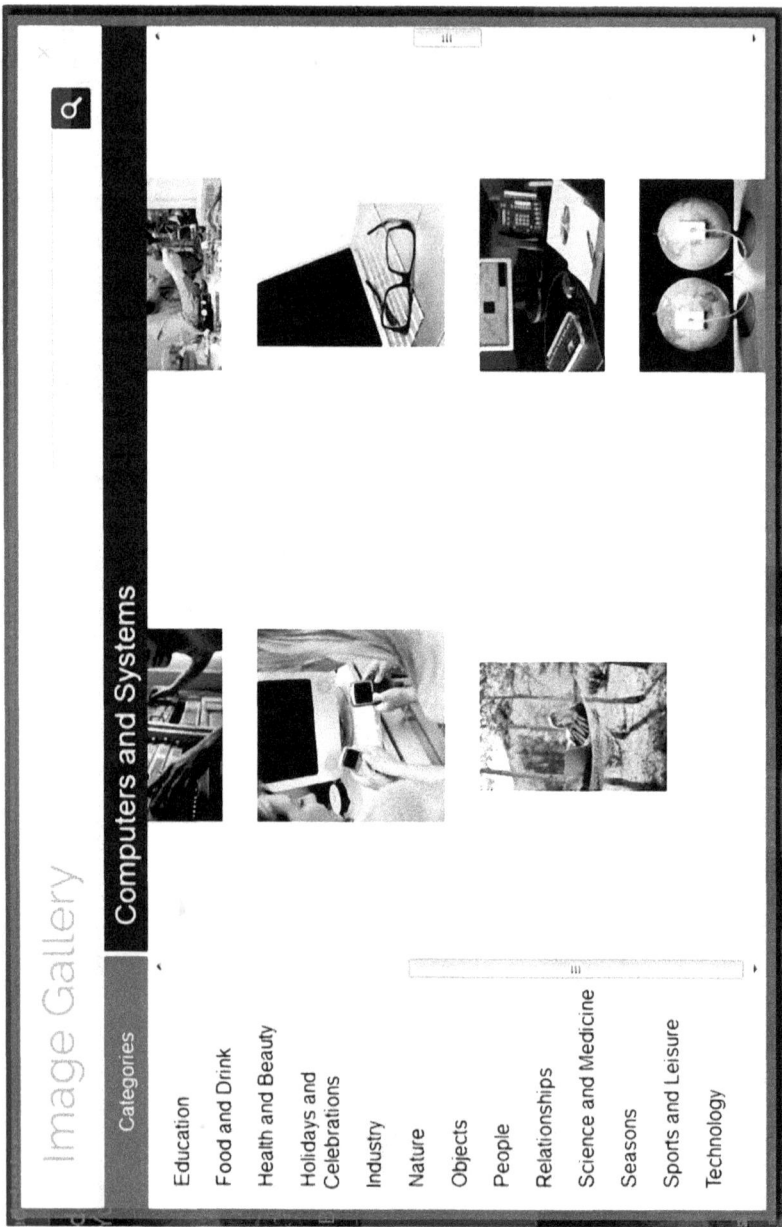

Notice there are many photographs to choose from in each section of each major category. KDP does a good job with providing a nice selection of workable images for you to use for your cover.

Once you've selected your image for the cover the gallery will give you complete details about the image.

On the next page you will see several possibilities for you
selected image plus four other possibilities that do not
include your selected image. Select the one you prefer
and you will be able to edit it afterwards.

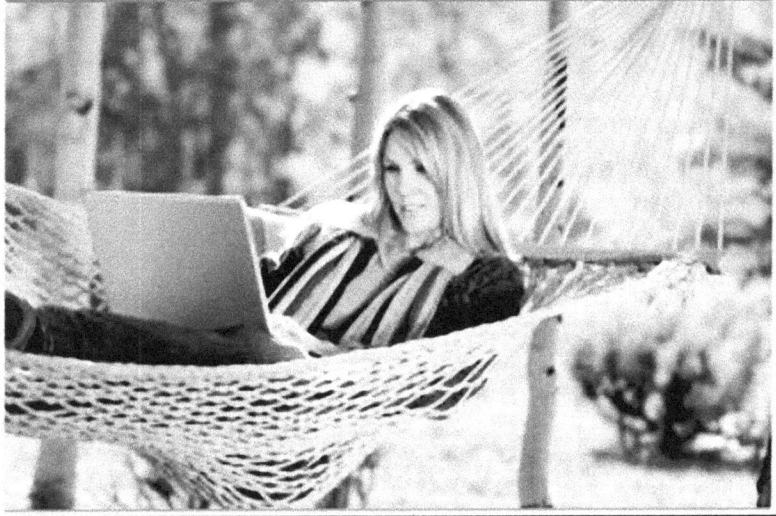

Independently Publish Your Ebooks

How To Sell on Kindle, iTunes, Barnes & Noble, Kobo, Flipkart, Clickbank, and Your Own Ebook Store

A. WILLIAM BENITEZ

This was my selection before I edited it.

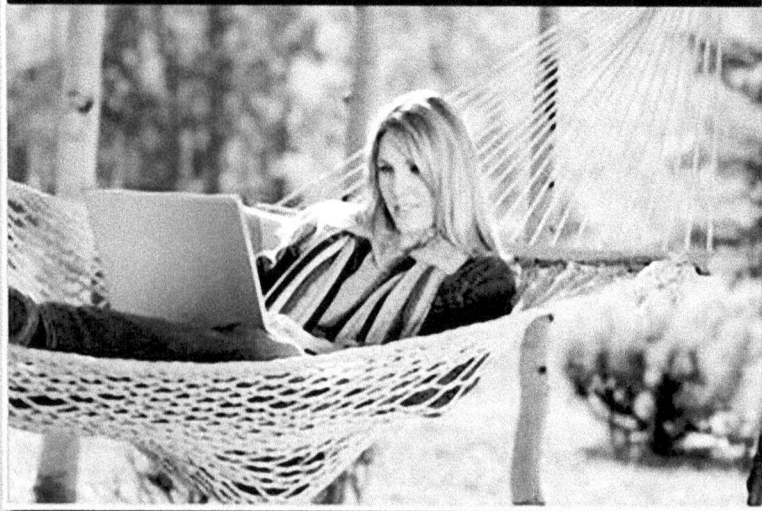

Independently
Publish Your
Ebooks

How To Sell on Kindle, iTunes, Barnes & Noble, Kobo,
Flipkart, Clickbank, and Your Own Ebook Store

A. WILLIAM BENITEZ

This is how it looked after I edited it.

Independently Publish Your Ebooks

How To Sell on Kindle, iTunes, Barnes & Noble, Kobo, Flipkart, Clickbank, and Your Own Ebook Store

A. WILLIAM BENITEZ

Save & Submit

This is the preview where you can enlarge any section to view it or you can click on Save and Submit.

Independently Publish Your Ebooks

Step 1	Step 2
Your book	**Rights & Pricing**
i In progress	*i* Not Started...

Once you Save and Submit your will be taken to the next step for creating you ebook which is Rights and Pricing as listed above.

Creating A Cover Yourself

This is an entirely different and much more complex thing but I decided to cover it in detail for those of you with the skills to carry it off.

Instead of just detailing the instructions for an ebook cover I decided to include instructions and screen shots that can be used for both ebook and print book covers. The only difference is that for ebooks you need only create the front page of the book cover. Print books require at least the front page and the back page and most times a spine. It's a lot more work and considerably more information but will add to the value of this book.

The details and screen shots in this book are from a cover I created for a book on self publishing that I published recently. The cover was created using PhotoPlus X4 an excellent graphic application by Serif a British software company. Even though I own Photoshop, I used PhotoPlus because it works well and is inexpensive.

At this writing, PhotoPlus X4 is available from Amazon.com for under $25.00 in either download or disk format but that could vary over time. This is a great tool for creating book covers but it is capable of much more including:

If you have the budget definitely consider Photoshop because it is an excellent graphic software. Even though it cost over $600 now, you can get it from Adobe Creative for only $10 per month.

  *Editing any photo in a myriad of ways

  *Add creative effects to any photograph.

  *Portrait retouching

  *You can work on RAW photos

  *Even works on videos

So, for a small price you get a tool that will easily handle all your cover work and many other photo related tasks.

Of course, a third option, hiring an artist to create a cover for you, is always available. Check out the rest of this chapter for ways to do it yourself and then decide how you want to handle your own book cover.

The image on the next page shows the entire workspace for PhotoPlus X4. All the screen shots that follow were created and then copied from this workspace.

PhotoPlus X4 is a reasonably priced, high quality, graphics editing and creation tool that will serve you during the creation of any book project.

It is possible to still get PhotoPlus X4 from some sources at a bargain price even though I haven't seen it for a while. However, as mentioned before, PhotoPlus X5, a newer version was available at Amazon when I wrote this book for only $25. A great bargain for this software that comes with excellent help files and the Serif company website includes helpful information and a community of users willing to help.

This screen shot was placed in the vertical position to make it large enough to see the details.

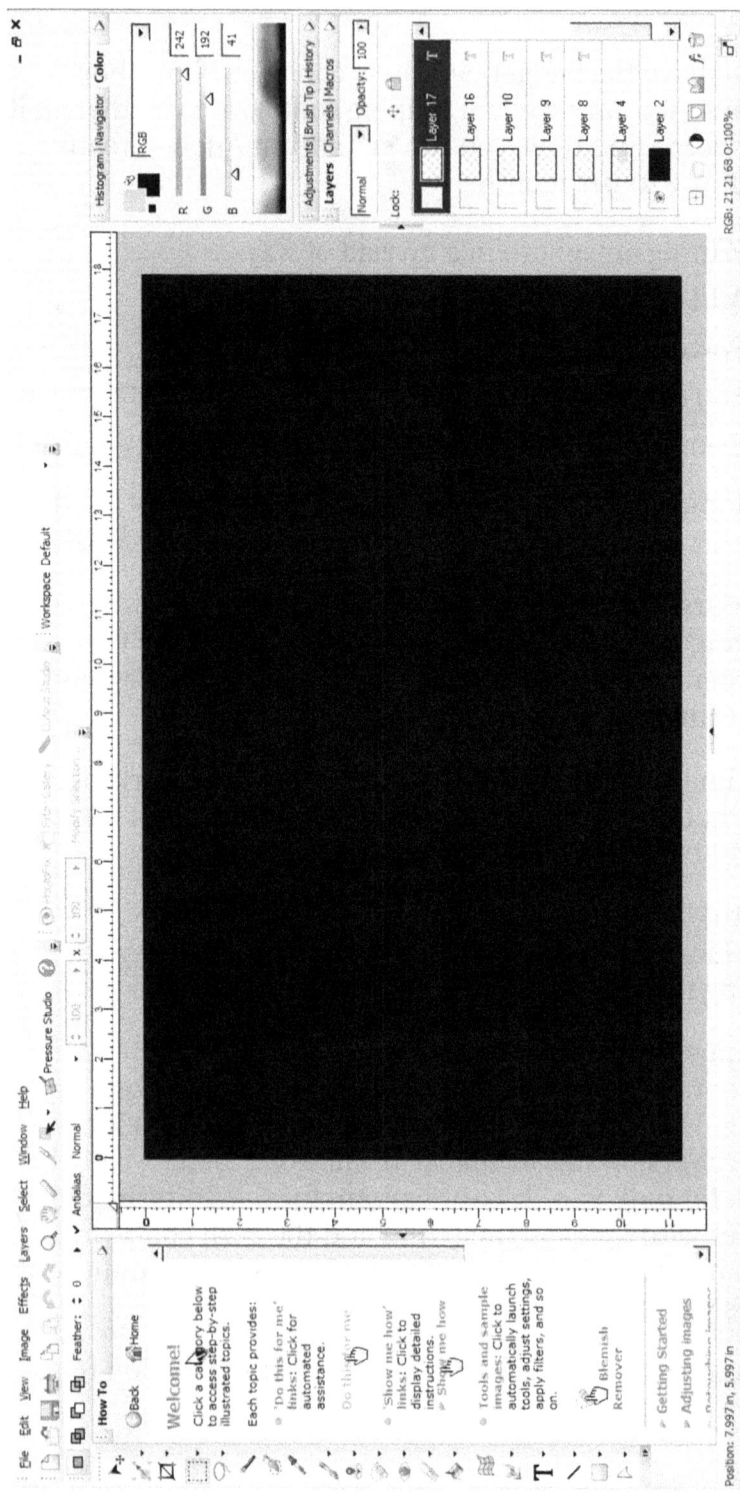

The Book Size

Before beginning a cover you must know the size of your book. In addition to the width and height of the book, you should know the number of pages. Once these dimensions are established, go to the Createspace web site and download a book cover template. This makes the job of creating the cover much simpler.

In this book the instructions do not involve a template because the book size is 8.5 inches by 11 inches and the largest template available from Createspace at the time of this writing was 8 inches by 10 inches. However, the steps for creating your cover with PhotoPlus X4 (or Photoshop if you have it) are the same except that you would begin by opening the template instead of creating a new image as outlined in these instructions.

One final note before we begin creating the cover with PhotoPlus X4. There is an excellent graphics application available free and capable of doing everything that PhotoPlus X4 or Photoshop can do related to covers. That application is called GIMP. Gimp can be downloaded free at: http://www.gimp.org/downloads/.

For the cover of a print book it's best to use a template. I get my templates from Createspace the company I recommend for POD printing. If you are not using a template then you must make some calculations before creating the initial image for the cover making the job much more complex but still doable.

For an ebook you don't need to use a template but you do need to adhere to some minimum sizes for your cover.

Kindle give specific instructions for the dimensions of cover files that you upload for any ebook you wish to publish with Kindle. They are as follows:

File Types

Kindle Direct Publishing currently accepts only JPG and TIFF files for cover images:

Dimensions

The ideal size of your cover art must have a height/width ratio of at least 8:5 which means your cover should be at least 5 inches wide and 8 inches tall. In pixels, this means the shortest side should be at least 625 pixels, and the longest side should be at least 1000 pixels. These are minimum dimensions and your cover can be larger but they won't accept any images larger than 10,000 pixels on the longest side and files cannot be larger than 50 MB.

Unlike print cover files which must be 300 pixels per inch, ebook cover files should be saved with 72 pixels per inch.

Below you see the background for the cover described in this book.

Let's go over the background size again for clarity. The size of the book described is 8.5 X 11 inches. This would make the background 17.75 X 11.25 inches. This is how that breaks down. The front and back covers will be 8.5 X 11 so for the background to cover both it must be 17 inches wide. The spine, based on the number of pages calculates to .50 inch. That makes the background 17.5 inches. Finally, you must add .125 inch to each side for the bleed which adds .25 inch total making the width of the background 17.75. Adding .25 inch to the 11 inch height gives you a cover height of 11.25 and adds .125 inch bleeds to the top and bottom of the cover.

All this work would be necessary for a print book but for your ebook you only need to make certain that your background meets the minimum sizes described on the previous page.

Note: If you plan to submit your ebook to Smashwords, then your cover image will have to be at least 1400 pixels across the shortest size or they won't accept it.

Once you have the size worked out you must be sure that you set the correct color for the background since this will be the base color of your cover.

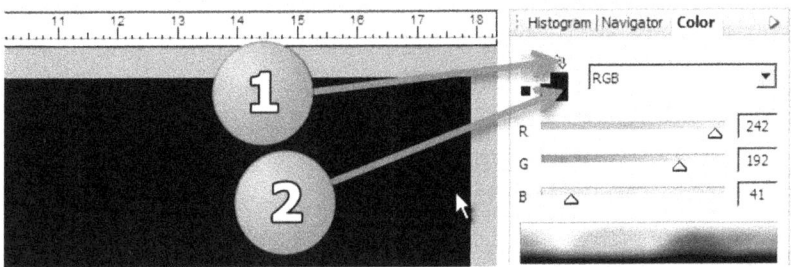

Number 2 above points to the background color. To change it to the correct, dark blue color, you click on the curved arrow and the colors are reversed. You can do this for each layer to maintain the colors you choose.

Once you have completed the background, you are ready to start adding the various objects and text to your cover.

For ease of working with the various objects and text it is critical to create a new layer for each. Usually, you will have to create a new layer for each object manually but each time you begin a new text location, a layer will be created automatically. In the screen shot below you can see the rectangular selection tool icon with the basic instructions in the pop up menu.

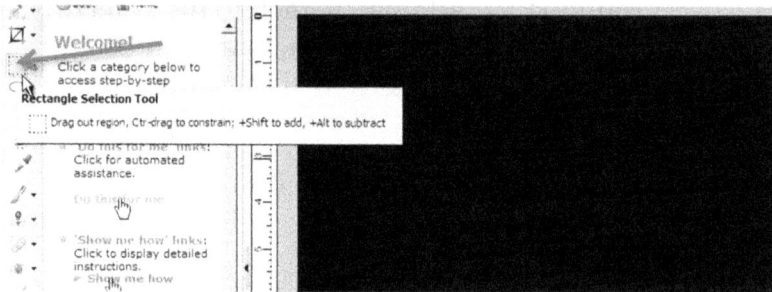

The second screen shot on the next page shows the first shape that I created. The size of the shape is actually 6 inches wide by 6.5 inches high. Shapes are created by placing the small plus sign anywhere on the background, holding the left mouse button and dragging it to the final point. Be sure to create a layer first so it's not essential to place the shape in its correct location. The important thing is to use the rulers to make certain the shape is the correct size. Once the shape has been completed it has to be filled with the correct color and dragged to its correct location. You can do those things in any order. I usually fill with the correct color as shown on this screen shot and then move the shape.

On this cover I only use two colors, the foreground and the background. For the same effect you need only select either one of these colors as covered on a previous screen shot. Once you have clicked the Flood Fill Tool as shown on the next page, you just move the cursor within the shape and click. The color will appear as shown in the bottom screen shot on the next page. Now you're ready to move the shape.

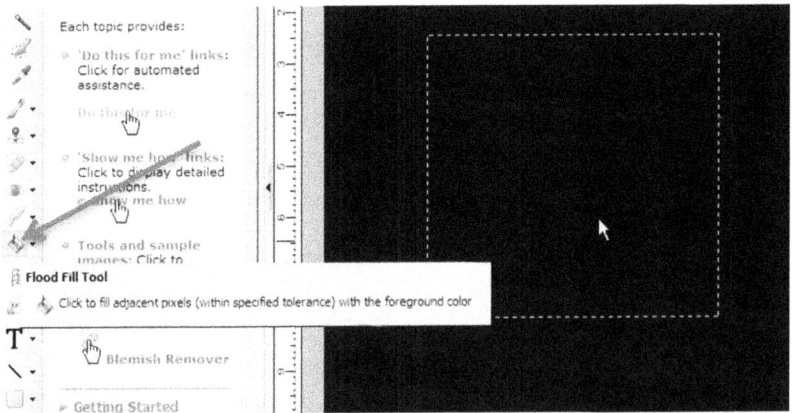

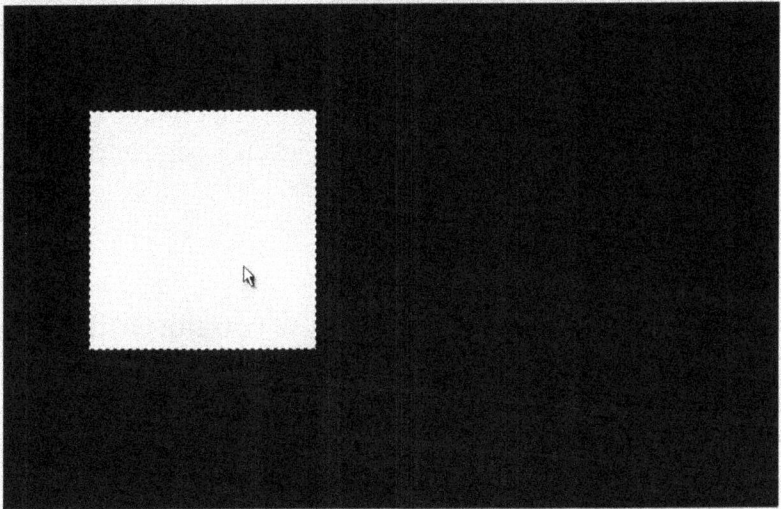

Notice that the shape is still not in the correct location. However, the shape was created on an independent layer. This allows me to move it to any location on the background without considering any other shape or object. In addition to moving a shape around to whatever location you choose, you can also move it above or below other objects or shapes as long as they are all on separate layers. This gives you great design flexibility.

The next step is to move the shape to the correct location on the background. Two things to remember when doing this. The first is to use the top and side rulers to control the location. The second is to remember that this first placement need not be perfect. Since the shape is on an independent layer, it can be moved at any time by selecting the layer and then using the move tool as shown below.

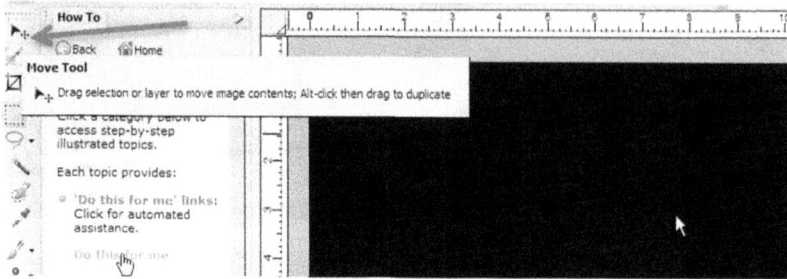

Use the rulers on the top and side of the main screen of PhotoPlus to identify the places where the shapes should be located. The ruler on top guides you to the horizontal location and the ruler at the left guides you to the vertical location.

The location of the plus sign of the move tool is always shown in the top and bottom rulers so you can easily maintain control of the exact location of the shape on your cover. You can move the shape slowly to its correct location and then continue your design. Remember that this location is not necessarily permanent. If you change the design or merely wish to move the shape, simply select the layer and the move tool and then you are free to change the location of the shape.

As you have probably noticed by now, creating a cover involves making many choices. I prefer to add all the shapes to the background before beginning the text. In the screen shot below you will see the second shape added. It was added to the background in exactly the same manner as the first shape except that it is a different size and is located in a different place. However, it is also on an independent layer that allows me to move it as needed.

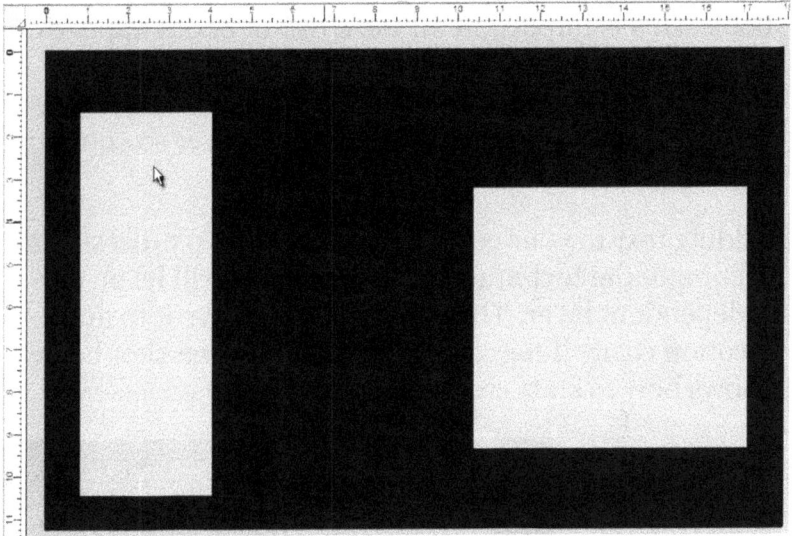

After all the shapes are in place, I proceed with the text. This is a critically important part of the cover and advance planning is essential. You should know exactly what you want your cover to convey to potential buyers.

The most important thing is the title of the book and that is handled in more detail in Chapter Five. The major consideration at this point is the font size for the title of the book and the subtitle. Remember that your book cover will be dramatically reduced in size when displayed on a web site and on Amazon. Choosing too small a font will make the title almost impossible to read when the book is displayed for sale.

The same goes for the subtitle. Even though it won't be as large as the title, it should still be readable on the thumbnail size images that appear on web sites. This is also the time to make certain that your subtitle conveys clearly the content of your book. This is especially critical for a how-to book.

Don't ignore the rest of the information on the front and rear cover. Notice on the cover of this book that it is easy to determine exactly what you will learn by reading the book. This is important on the cover of books appearing in bookstores where information that clearly explains the content will make a difference. With ebooks all the information appears only on the front cover so you must create the title and subtitle carefully.

Adding text to your cover is a multiple step process. Each section of the text must be handled so it will be on an independent layer. This allows you to move it to any location easily if necessary. This first screen shot below shows how to start creating the text.

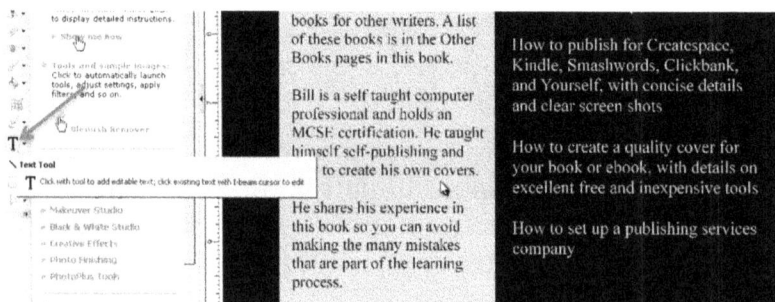

After clicking the text tool icon, you move the cursor to the location of the text, click the mouse and then begin typing. Don't worry if the text is placed correctly. Each time you begin to input text, a new layer is created. If your text is not exactly where you want it you simply click on the move tool and move the text or the layer to the correct location.

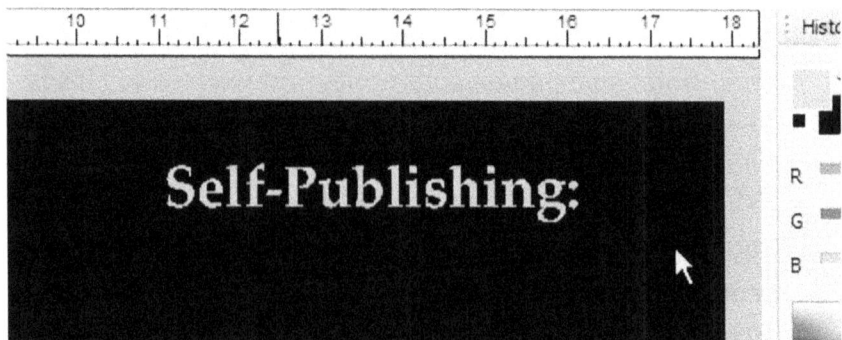

Above is the title text. Notice the large size of the font even in the reduced size of this screen shot. The subtitle goes right below it and is only slightly smaller than the title so it is also easy to read.

You can proceed to create all the different text sections for your cover. Not all covers require as much text as this one. It was important to me to convey as much information as possible about the book. That may not be helpful for other kinds of books but it is important with a how-to book.

Before showing you the final cover for this book, I still have one more shape and two photographs to add. I will describe the addition of those objects and then show you the final cover.

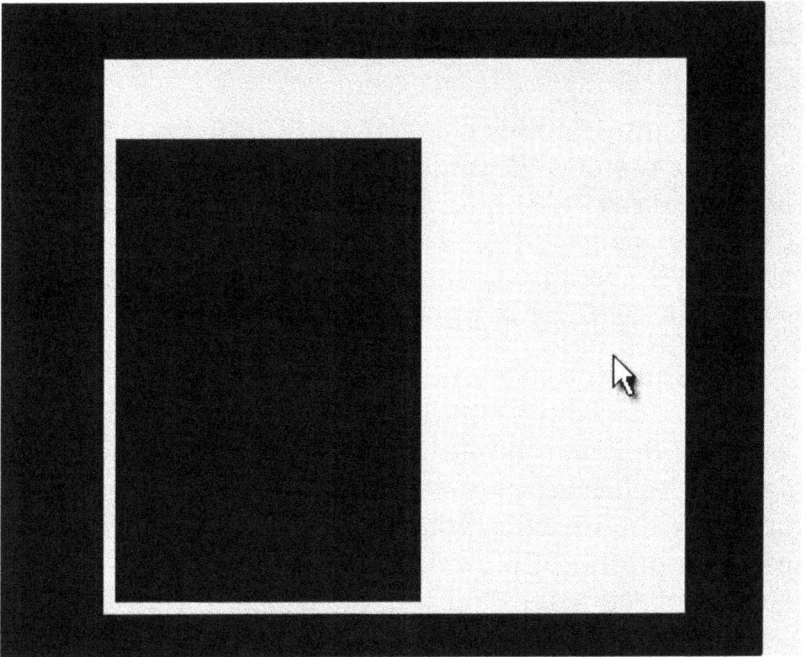

This is the final shape to be placed on the background. Notice that this object is the same color as the background. This is part of the design of my book cover.

This shape is placed so that the left side and the bottom are the same size from the edge of the larger shape.

In addition to this spacing, a much larger spacing is left above the shape for a large line of text. On the right hand side of the shape there is room for more text about the book.

This is a design concept that I developed for two of my previous how-to books. Those two book were in the 8 inch by 10 inch size instead of 8.5 inches by 11 inches of this book but the design is basically the same.

This new shape will serve as the frame for a photograph that I had taken especially for this purpose. The photograph will be placed in this shape with even borders around it. The important thing to remember is that this shape is created exactly like the other two except for the size.

Placing photographs is handled a little differently but one thing remains the same, you want to add the photograph as a new layer so that it can be moved and controlled should changes arises. I repeat the caution about layers because it is the only easy way to create a cover. The cover for this book has more than 20 layers.

The next step is to place the images on the cover. To do that you must edit the images to make certain they are at least 300 dpi (dots per inch) in resolution and the correct size for the cover. It is not a good idea to increase or reduce the size of a photograph when placing it on a cover for printing. These changes tend to have an adverse effect on the quality of the image.

To make the image for this cover the correct size, I calculated the size of the blue shape where I was going to place the photograph and then deducted .25 inch from the top and the side and that gave me the correct size for the photograph. Once placed on the blue shape, there would be a .125 inch (1/8 inch) border of blue around the photograph. You can adjust the size for your photographs accordingly.

Once the image is the correct size and resolution for the cover, use the rectangle tool to capture a copy of the photograph. Then either select Edit and Copy or use the Ctrl, C keys on your keyboard to capture a copy of the photograph.

Now, return to the main cover workspace and select Edit again and this time select Paste. Make absolutely certain that you select Paste As a New Layer. This will paste the photograph at the upper left hand corner. Then select the move tool and move the photograph to the correct location. This will work perfectly for every photograph you need to place on your cover.

Should your photograph size be incorrect, simply select Edit, Undo and resize the photograph. Until you become proficient with PhotoPlus X4, it may take several tries. The photo below shows the capture lines it's not the final.

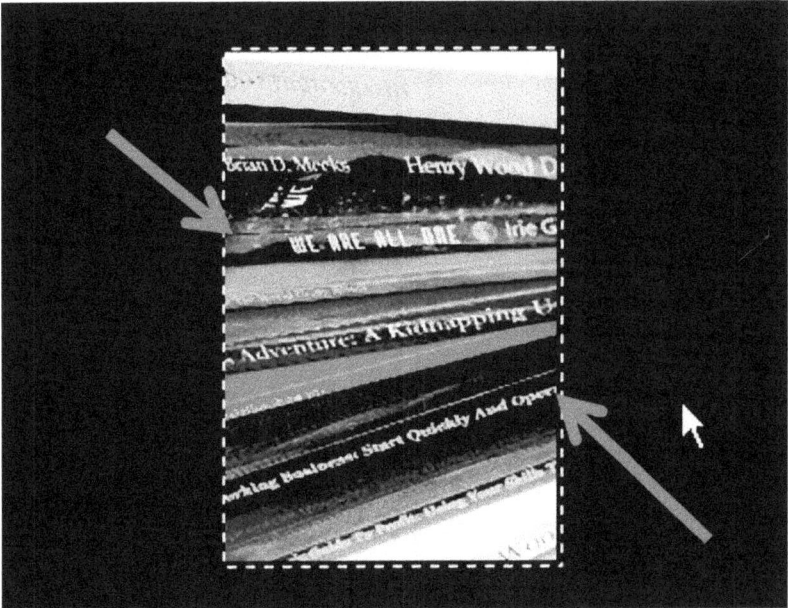

To copy and paste the photographs into the cover use the Menu icons as shown in the screen shots below.

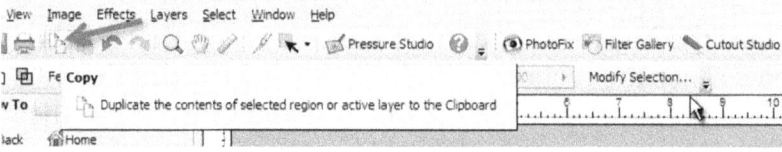

Remember, as shown below, always Paste As New Layer so you will have complete control over the positioning of the photograph, shape, or object. Once the layer is moved and the photo is placed in its correct location it will look as it does in the screen shot below.

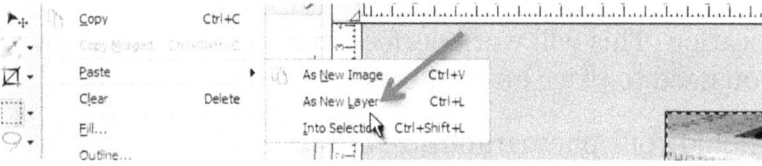

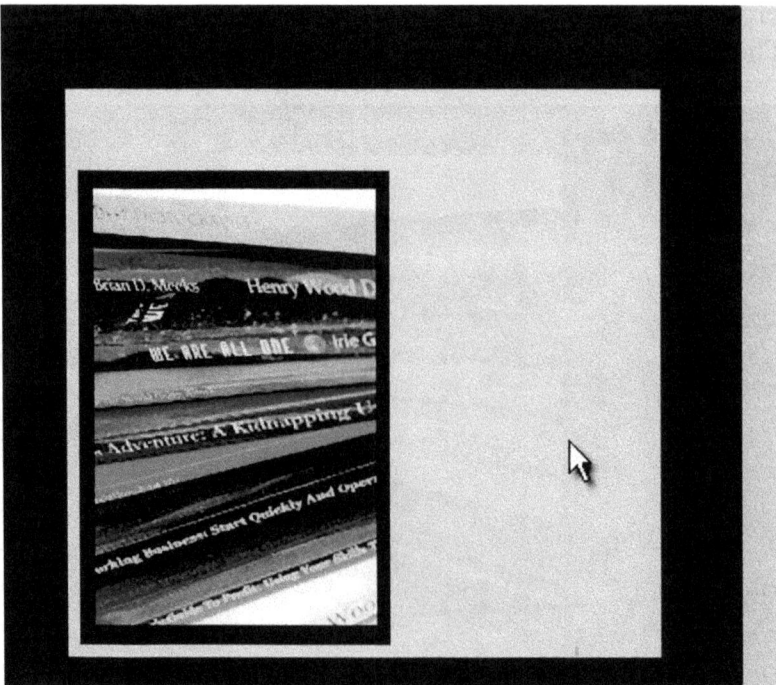

Creating Text For The Spine

The process of creating text for the spine can be difficult and is unnecessary for ebooks but I'm including it as a help for those doing print books. The first step is to create lines to identify the exact location of the spine so you will know where to type the text. Be sure to make new layers for each line, object, or text created.

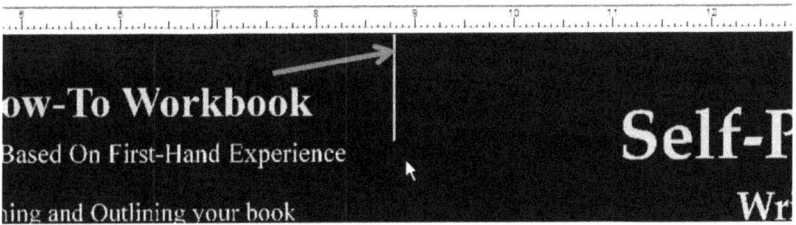

Each of the lines should be drawn from the top of the cover to the bottom. Use the ruler at the top to place the lines in the correct locations. The space between the lines must be the size that you determine by using the calculations from the Createspace web site. These lines will serve as a guide to type the spine content.

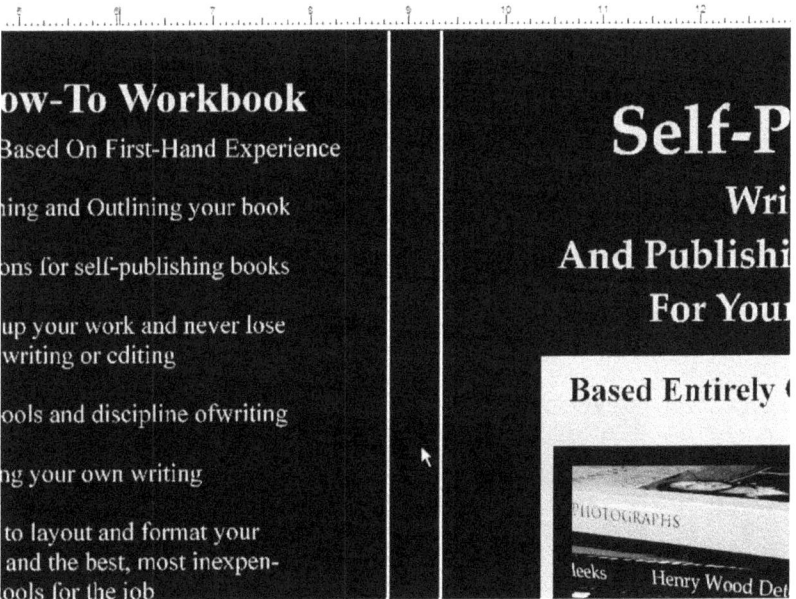

After drawing the two lines using the line tool, you must rotate the entire cover so that you can type the spine text. You must rotate it counter clockwise so the spine writing will be correctly oriented. The screen shots on the next page show how to rotate the cover and the rotated view blank and with the spine text typed.

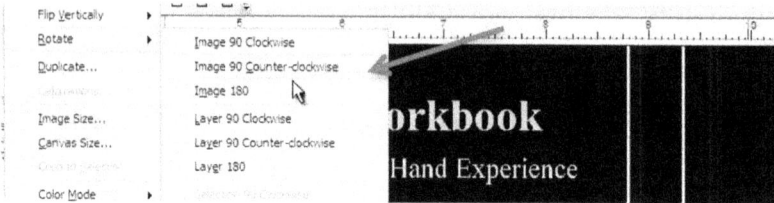

As shown in the screen shot above, rotating the image is a simple task. Just click on Image and then Rotate and then choose Image 90 Counter-clockwise. This will place the image in the correct position for typing in the spine text.

When typing the text leave at least .75 inch from the top and the bottom of the cover. Simply start typing at the left as you normally do and type the title of the book. Unless the subtitle is very short, only the title will fit in this space.

Next leave several spaces and type the last name of the author. You may type the full name but standard practice is to include only the last name in the spine. Once the name is typed, put the cursor in front of the name and either press the space button to move the name closer to the bottom or backspace to move it away from the bottom.

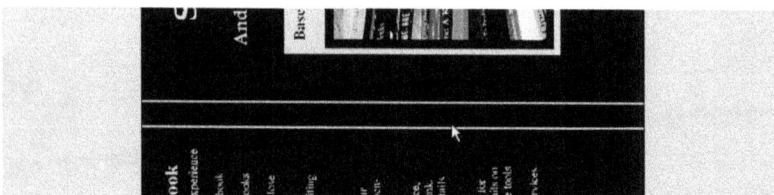

When you type the spine text, as with all the other text sections you created, a new layer is created allowing you to adjust the spine text to be perfectly centered in the spine.

Notice on the screen shot below that the spine text matches all the other text in font choice and color. This is part of my design for the covers of all my how-to books. You can add other things to the spine including a small logo or some other design. Just make certain that it isn't too large so that it overlaps or gets too close to the corner of spine.

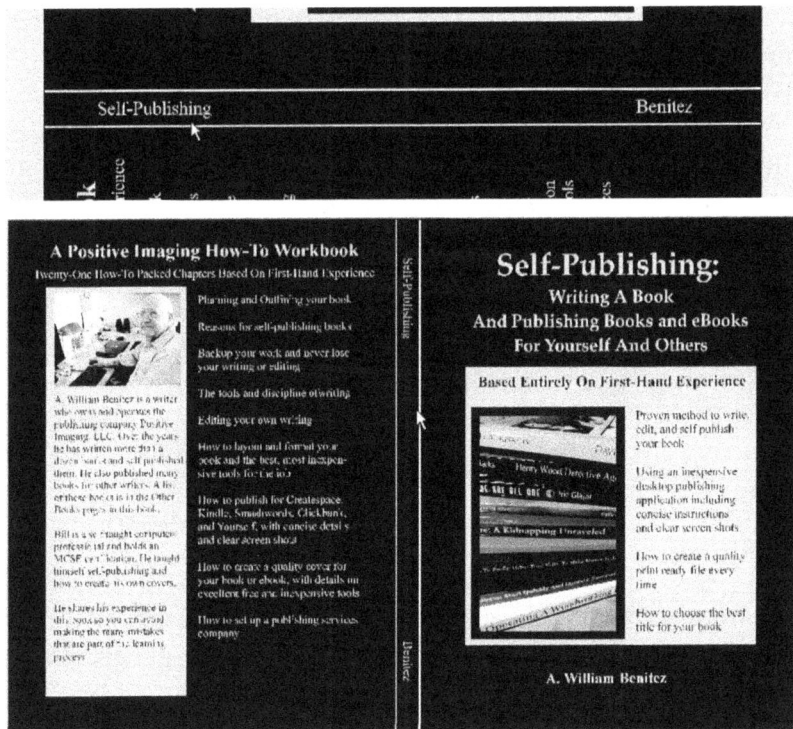

After the image is rotated back to its correct position, the lines are still visible and must be removed from the image. This is easy to do by simply clicking on the small eye in each line layer. You can see on the screen shot on the next page that one of the lines is gone and the arrow is pointing to where I click to get rid of the second line.

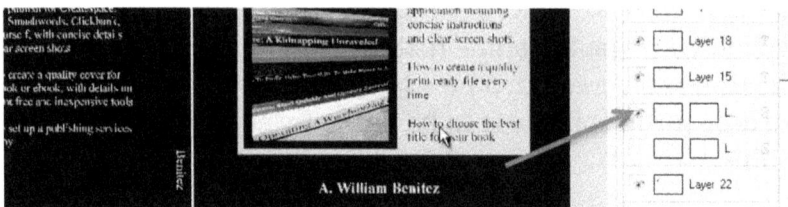

Clicking on the eye not only gives you control of the visibility of this line but this also works on every layer in the photo. So, you can turn off all the layers or leave them all on as you choose. Working with layers provides great flexibility when creating covers or any other photo projects.

On the next page I have included the entire cover and rotated it on the page so it is viewed in a larger format. In this chapter every step for creating a cover using PhotoPlus X4 has been covered. However, it is important to develop a familiarity with the software because this will help you to learn how to create better covers or other projects.

The same work can be done with Photoshop at a cost of $600.00 plus or with GIMP at no cost but I like working with PhotoPlus X4 and it is a bargain.

On the next page is the entire cover after it was completed. It is turned vertical to make it easier to see at this smaller size.

Remember, that this is a full size, front and back, cover for a print book. When making a cover for an ebook the spine and the back cover are unnecessary so the job is much simpler.

Self-Publishing:
Writing A Book
And Publishing Books and eBooks
For Yourself And Others

Based Entirely On First-Hand Experience

Proven method to write, edit, and self publish your book

Using an inexpensive desktop publishing application including concise instructions and clear screen shots

How to create a quality print ready file every time

How to choose the best title for your book

A. William Benitez

A Positive Imaging How-To Workbook

Twenty-One How-To Packed Chapters Based On First-Hand Experience

Planning and Outlining your book

Reasons for self-publishing books

Backup your work and never lose your writing or editing

The tools and discipline of writing

Editing your own writing

How to layout and format your book and the best, most inexpensive tools for the job

How to publish for Createspace, Kindle, Smashwords, Clickbank, and Yourself, with concise details and clear screen shots

How to create a quality cover for your book or ebook, with details on excellent free and inexpensive tools

How to set up a publishing services company

A. William Benitez is a writer who owns and operates the publishing company Positive Imaging, LLC. Over the years he has written more than a dozen books and self published many of them. He also published many books for other writers. A list of these books is in the Other Books pages in this book.

Bill is a self-taught computer professional and holds an MCSE certification. He taught himself self-publishing and how to create his own covers.

He shares his experience in this book so you can avoid making the many mistakes that are part of the learning process.

Notes

8

Publishing Ebooks for the Kindle

Amazon Kindle is a great market for almost all ebooks. It can be a secondary ebook market for your paperback books, or it can be the sole market for your ebooks. Listing your ebooks on Amazon Kindle works great. If you begin with a paperback that is listed on Amazon and then publish an ebook version, both of them will be available on the same sales page, so your prospects have the opportunity to purchase either one.

Because of the direct connection with Amazon, Kindle is the ideal place to publish ebooks. When you publish your eBook on Kindle it automatically appears for sale on Amazon.com. The Kindle publishing program is called KDP (Kindle Direct Publishing) and they provide complete instructions and all the tools you need to convert your book file to a Kindle eBook file and begin earning up to 70% commission on every sale of your eBook. There is one catch to this arrangement, you must list your ebook exclusively with Amazon for the first 90 days. If you list your ebook with any other seller during the initial period, you will only receive a 35% royalty on each ebook sold.

Kindle Lending Library

In addition to the normal sales channels, Kindle has created a new lending library that while controversial has the potential to increase an author's profit on ebooks. As part of this Lending Library Kindle has created a fund that begans with a half million dollars and increased to over six million to pay for the use of the books in the Lending Library. It may not mean much for some books but for popular books it can mean a windfall in addition to sales.

Joining the Lending Library program, called KDP Select, in no way affects your commission on books sold through KDP. Instead, it helps you to make money from readers who seldom purchase books. KDP Select can expose you to more customers and can increase your profits. You can get complete details about the KDP Select program at Amazon.com.

Creating a Kindle eBook

There are several easy to follow methods. One involves creating the manuscript using Microsoft Word and creating a .doc file. Remember that the newer versions of Microsoft Word create .docx files by default and these will not work well because of additional built-in code that may create issues when converted. To create a .doc file, which is best for this purpose, you have to choose **Save As** instead of just Save and save your manuscript as a .doc file. This doc file is the one to use for your formatting.

There are several important things to remember in creating this .doc file. Start at the KDP web site by becoming a member. It's free and gives you full access to some great tools and lots of free advice.

Kindle converts many formats to the final format for ebooks. These include Word, ePub, plain Text, Mobi-Pocket, and HTML. There several ways to arrive at the final Kindle format and many companies are willing to handle the entire process for you for a fee ranging from quite reasonable to unreasonable. Since the KDP site is so informative, this book will only cover the one method I use to create the final file for conversion. This method works consistently and should work well for you and preclude the need to hire someone to do the conversion.

You can prepare the final file for KDP using any version of Word as long as you use the .doc format. Just follow the steps below to prepare the final file.

One – Use the **Normal** template only and avoid creating any unusual styles. These will present problems for the conversion. Authors sometimes attempt to format their book by creating complex styles while typing the draft. Keep it as simple as possible.

Two – Make certain that you are saving the file in the .doc format not the .docx format to avoid complications to the conversion process.

Three – You can use indentations, bold text, italics, and headings but avoid bullet points, special fonts, headers, and footers because they won't transfer and the final result will not look good.

Four – Use a page break after each chapter to keep the text from running together in the Kindle reader. Remember, there are no specific pages in a Kindle reader since the user can alter the size of the font and can also read in both the vertical and horizontal position which alters the length of the lines. A page break will push the beginning of a chapter to a new page in the Kindle.

Note: The importance of the page break in creating a professional looking Kindle book can't be overemphasized. To create a page break in Word simply click the Insert Menu at the top and then select Page Break.

Five – The Kindle automatically indents the first line of each paragraph and it displays the text fully justified so you don't have to handle that aspect of the formatting. However, if you want a specific indentation at the beginning of a paragraph, do not use tab spacing. This does not convert into the Kindle format. To control the indentation use the **Paragraph Formatting** to set the first line indent.

Six – You can use images but it's important to center them on the page and to control their location using page breaks. For example, if you want the picture to have a full page, place a page break after the text and then after the image to devote the full page to the image. If you would like an image set at the beginning of a chapter, put a page break at the end of the previous chapter, place the image and then use the Enter key to add one or two line spaces after the image and follow that with the rest of the chapter text.

Seven – Use .jpg images exclusively and **Insert** them into the manuscript. Remember not to copy and paste them into the manuscript. Even though the Kindle readers only see images in 16 shades of gray, leave the pictures in color because Kindle Fire and other readers can see the colors and they can be viewed in color using the free Kindle apps for PCs, MACs, iPad, iPhone, and Android.

Eight – Like a paperback, Kindle books can have a Title Page, Copyright Page, Dedication, Preface, Prologue, etc. You should have at least a title page, and each of these pages should be separated by page breaks to make them individual pages in the Kindle book.

There are several things that should be added to your Kindle book to make it a much better product. These are not required to upload your book and shouldn't be used for short and simple books. However, longer and more complex books benefit from having a Table of Contents.

The easiest tool for creating an Active Table of Contents is Microsoft Word. If you are already using Word to create your manuscript, then it's easy to begin the process. Before starting to work on the Active Table of Contents, use the Save As command to save the completed manuscript under a different name. You can simply add the numeral 1 at the end of the file name and save it. Then any changes you make to the file will not affect your completed manuscript just in case you encounter difficulties while creating the Active Table of Contents or any other aspect of the file.

Microsoft offers precisely detailed instructions on how to create an Active Table of Contents with any version of Microsoft Word. You can read or print out these complete instructions at:

http://support.microsoft.com/kb/285059

An Active Table of Contents is a great tool for a How-To book because it makes it easy for the reader to choose various topics to read at any time.

Naturally, your book can also include Back Matter which are things like a bibliographies, appendices, glossaries, or notes.

Once you have completed your draft, edited it fully, and deem it a final manuscript, you are ready to upload to Kindle. Remember, the file must be in the .doc format not .docx.

OpenOffice Word Processing Suite

OpenOffice creates an odt file as the default but is also capable of creating a .doc file if you use **Save As** instead of just **Save**. While this should allow you to work with these files, it doesn't always work perfectly for this work. OpenOffice Writer is an excellent application but if you choose to use it you should consider using it in conjunction with another excellent application called Jutoh that allows you to convert odt files to Kindle ready files. Unlike OpenOffice, Jutoh is not a free application. It costs $39.00 and is well worth the price. However, since you can convert files for the Kindle with free applications provided by KDP, there is no need to pay for an application. It is simply another option for OpenOffice users.

NOTE: When creating an Active Table of Contents with OpenOffice I suggest you use the bookmark/hyperlink method. After your manuscript is completed, type up the list of chapters for the Table of Contents. Go back to the heading of each chapter, highlight each of them and make them bookmarks. Then return to your Table of Contents and individually select each chapter title and highlight it. Then select Hyperlink and create a hyperlink to the appropriate chapter heading. This will give you a fully functional Active Table of Contents.

9

Publishing eBooks For Smashwords
(iTunes, Barnes & Noble, Kobo, Flipkart, etc.)

The name Smashwords may not strike an inspirational note at first glance, unless you remember that Smash also has a positive meaning. Take a few moments to check out the details on the Smashwords site and it may sound too good to be true. As it turns out, everything on the site is quite accurate.

The success of the Kindle rekindled (no pun intended) interest in ebooks. Their recent report indicating that they were selling 1.8 Kindle books to every paperback book proves that it would be unwise to ignore ebooks.

> *I had already begun reformatting my wife Barbara's children's chapter book for the Kindle when I heard about Smashwords. I immediately changed over and now have it published as an ebook with Smashwords in addition to the Kindle version. It simply made sense because Smashwords is a leading independent ebook publisher, distributor and aggregator with well over 400,000 titles already published. As an aggregator Smashwords is a one stop place for having your ebooks available to many distributors including iTunes, Barnes & Noble Nook, Kobo, etc.*

There is no question that Smashwords is an excellent path to getting an ebook published and noticed. Please remember to read the format requirements before submitting your books for acceptance. Some have had difficulty successfully formatting their book even though it's not that difficult. The procedure for preparing a Word document for Smashwords is almost identical to Kindle's except as it relates to the Active Table of Contents. On Kindle book the Table of Contents may be based on Headings that are used to create an interactive Table of Contents. This doesn't work for Smashwords.

With Smashwords you create the Table of Contents, then create Bookmarks for each item listed on the Table of Contents. Finally, you create Hyperlinks on the Table of Contents to the individual Bookmarks. It takes an additional step but it simple to do.

Fortunately, Smashword's helpful owner, Mark Coker, is clearly someone who knows how to create comprehensive how-to information. You can download an invaluable Style Guide and follow it carefully so your ebooks will get accepted the first time, everytime.

If you've created ebooks, even for the Kindle, you'll find Smashwords unique. You submit only one properly formatted manuscript and Smashwords, using a computer affectionately called the meatgrinder, turns it into a multi-format ebook that can be purchased and read on many platforms. This multi-format availability is based on a two-step process.

Step one takes place immediately when your manuscript is accepted as properly formatted. It then becomes available to the public in the following formats: Html and Javascript for online reading, Kindle (mobi), ePub for stanza readers and many others, Pdf and Rtf for computers, lrf for Sony Readers, Pdb for Palm reading devices, and plain text. Think about that for a moment, once your manuscript is accepted, it is available in all those formats and immediately downloadable. Remember, even though your Smashwords ebook can be read on Kindle, it is not listed on Amazon and that will affect sales.

There is nothing else you have to do other than get the word out about your ebook. Smashwords handles all the sales for you, creates a sampler version of your ebook, and you choose whether to provide from 20% to 50% of your ebook to potential customers before they buy. You can also create coupons for special deals, like a certain number of free copies or special discount for a certain time, to encourage sales. Smashwords also does a great deal of marketing for you by showing your other books, should you have more than one. Plus, they show your book when someone is searching for related topics similar to Amazon.

If you are a writer with several books, then your standard profile is fine. If you publish books for other writers, you have to join as a publisher. Either way, there are no fees to join and no cost to publish. Being a publisher is slightly more complex, but it allows you control of all your books. Depending on the arrangement, you will get between 70% and 85% of the income from the sale of your ebook.

Premium Level is the ultimate step in Smashwords, and it is a good idea to strive for this level. There are significant advantages and it's a little more difficult to get your manuscripts accepted at this level, but there is still no cost involved. The most important advantage of the Premium Level is that your ebooks become available for distribution on more markets including Apple (iPad and iPhone) Barnes and Noble within their Nook ebook format, and Droid. You don't have to attain Premium Level to be a Smashwords author, but it could make a significant difference in sales.

For those considering self-publishing, Smashwords is a perfect way to start. It's easy to create an acceptable manuscript using Word and you can make revisions and upload a revised copy at any time. It also helps you determine if your book is salable before making a larger investment. With the present trend towards ebooks, Smashwords is a good place for self-publishers.

Notes

10

Publishing eBooks Using Other Options

Kindle and Smashwords are not the only games in town for ebooks. Clickbank is a good place for .pdf based eBooks. You can use the same methods used for creating a print ready file except you would add a front and back cover file. Then the book is uploaded to Clickbank and if it is approved, they will sell it for you.

Clickbank

Clickbank provides a unique service in that they not only set up a place to store and sell your eBook, they also have thousands of affiliates who may decide to sell your eBook through their website to get a commission from the sale. You decide the amount of the commission you wish to pay and then place your eBook in the database. Any affiliate interested in selling your eBook obtains a link to use on their site and that link identifies them so when anyone buys the eBook using their link, you make a profit, and they collect a commission on the sale. If your ebook is on a popular topic and leaves a reasonable commission, it may be sold by hundreds of affiliates thereby multiplying your sales significantly without any effort on your part. You can learn all about Clickbank at their main web site: http://www.clickbank.com/

In addition to their informative home page, you will find a large collection of valuable articles to help you to use Clickbank successfully to sell your ebook and you could even sell other ebooks related to your topic by becoming a Clickbank affiliate.

Your Website

For any of you who already have websites set up and a list of potential buyers, you may consider handling everything yourself. You start by creating your ebook in the .pdf format. You can simply use the letter size, 8.5 X 11 commonly used, but I suggest separating yourself from the pack by creating your eBooks in the 5 X 7 size easily viewed on any device. Using a format in this size allows the reader to see one page at a time without scrolling.

Another positive thing for your eBooks in the .pdf format is to create an interactive table of contents to help readers who may know a great deal about the topic but just need some specific information.

You can make your eBooks even easier to use by adding links on each page. For example, each page can have a small button at the bottom for the next page, the previous page, going back to the table of contents. Or a Go To specific page which allows you to select a page in which you are interested. Unlike regular ebooks, pdf ebooks have individual pages and the font size can't be changed, so these additional features can be added and are appreciated. None of these things are essential, and they do require software capable of working within .pdf documents. While many believe that only Adobe makes such software, and at a quite high price, actually there are many companies that make software for this purpose at more reasonable prices including PDF Converter Professional 7 available at the link below where you can also download a free trial version to test for yourself.

http://www.nuance.com/products/pdf-converterprofessional7/index.htm

There are many free tools you can use to create .pdf files and office suites such as OpenOffice and Microsoft Office have built in tools to create .pdf files from the documents created with them. However, for editing and improving

.pdf files a program such as PDF Converter Professional 7 is invaluable.

The main advantage of selling your ebooks from your website is that all of the profits are yours. It's a significant advantage but requires you to have considerable skills and a payment process to collect for your sales. The skills involve creating a sales page for your book. You also need the skills to market your book by creating traffic to your website and conducting many other marketing activities beyond the scope of this book.

The payment process is not as complex as it sounds. For a minor fee, you can get set up with Paypal to collect for the sale of your book or ebook. With Paypal, you can even set up a shopping cart if you have several books or ebooks to sell. Get complete details about Paypal at their main website:

http://www.paypal.com

Another disadvantage of handling all your sales is that it requires you to get much more serious about running a business. You have to make arrangements to collect and pay the sales tax on your sales. You also have to set up your credit card payment process as previously indicated because sales aren't handled by a company like Click-bank, Amazon, or Smashwords, who would take care of everything and report to you on your income.

Notes

11

Creating A Web Site
To Market Your Ebook

Creating a website for your ebook is a critical part of marketing. Even though this book does not deal with the many details of marketing books, it does cover the important preparations required to begin marketing any book.

Even if you have no interest in selling your ebook, you almost certainly would like others to read it. A good web site will allow it to be found and read by others.

In this chapter you will find illustrations of many web sites with some details of how they were made and how they impact the marketing of books or ebooks.

Before beginning the illustrations it's important to have some idea of the many tools available to help you create your own web sites. Many of these tools perform quite well and are completely free. Others also perform well but must be purchased. Still others are quite easy to use but require a monthly financial commitment that can be difficult to cancel. Let's start with a brief list and then the details

WebPlus - This is a fine product from Serif, the same company that created PagePlus and PhotoPlus.

NVU and Kompozer - These two WYSIWYG web site creation applications are both free and easy to use.

Website Tonight - Is available free from many web hosting companies when you sign up with them to host your web site. More on hosting later in this chapter.

Yahoo Small Business - This service and other similar ones provide a one stop location for domain names, web hosting, and web site creation tools, all online and easy to use at a reasonable cost.

> *There are other ways to get a web site created and hosted but these are the only ones that I have used personally. I prefer to handle all aspects of the process myself but Yahoo provides a good service.*

Let's begin this section with illustrations of web sites created for a specific book.

It's Time For Children's Adventure Books

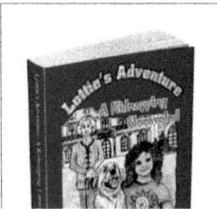

Lottie's Adventure

A Kidnapping Unraveled

"Lottie's Adventure: A Kidnapping Unraveled" is a vibrant chapter book mystery for preteens that emphasizes the importance of intergenerational communication and love as well as the immense value of thinking beyond cultural stereotypes. To develop a new moral code or vision, both these elements are crucial. Perhaps the most striking quality of "Lottie's Adventure: A Kidnapping Unraveled" is its powerful positive energy. Featuring a spunky 10-year-old Hispanic heroine, "Lottie's Adventure" keeps interest high and pages turning with exciting plot twists and turns and believable cliffhangers that just keep evolving. The author allows her characters to develop very naturally, with total authenticity. There are many excellent ideas embedded in the story, not the least of which is that people, even wise adults, can learn to admit they are wrong. "Lottie's Adventure"

Click on the Order Now button below

> *This web site was created for the children's adventure book my wife wrote back in 2007. It was one of my first experiences with POD. I shot the video of the granddaughter of a good friend talking about the book and it turned out well. This site was created with NVU.*

The cover drawing was done by a local artist and then I did quite a bit of Photoshop work on it to get the exact look that we wanted. I designed the cover and then scanned it and just put a flat picture of the cover on the site. Later, I found an artist who would take my flat drawing and make it into the book design that you see above for only twenty dollars.

The clock was something I found for free on the web and have used it on several web sites. The rest of the header is an animated file and the words Lottie's Adventure move slowly and continuously giving an scary effect.

The two black and white drawings were taken directly from the inside of the book which has a small drawing at the beginning of each chapter.

At first I hosted this web site with a popular hosting company and that worked fine but I found that I could save a lot of money by purchasing a hosting reseller arrangement with a company and then host all my sites for one small monthly payment.

This web site was created for the children's adventure book my wife wrote back in 2007. It was one of my first experiences with POD. I shot the video of the granddaughter of a good friend talking about the book and it turned out well. This site was created with NVU.

The cover drawing was done by a local artist and then I did quite a bit of Photoshop work on it to get the exact look that we wanted. I designed the cover and then scanned it and just put a flat picture of the cover on the site. Later, I found an artist who would take my flat drawing and make it into the book design that you see above for only twenty dollars.

The clock was something I found for free on the web and have used it on several web sites. The rest of the header is an animated file and the words Lottie's Adventure move slowly and continuously giving an scary effect.

The two black and white drawings were taken directly from the inside of the book which has a small drawing at the beginning of each chapter.

At first I hosted this web site with a popular hosting company and that worked fine but I found that I could save a lot of money by purchasing a hosting reseller arrangement with a company and then host all my sites for one small monthly payment.

The two web sites on the next page were created for books that were published by Positive Imaging, LLC, my company, but I didn't write them. The web sites were designed to serve as the press kit for this author.

The first page of these web sites are about the book and have a buy link for purchase. They also include a page about the author, and a press release page. The We Are All One site has its own domain but the Teach For Life site is a sub-domain of the Positive Imaging web site. That is a way to save the cost of hosting a second or third site.

On the next page is another web site made for a book that Positive Imaging, LLC published for another individual. That site plus the two above were all created with Web Plus X4, another excellent software application from Serif, the same British company that makes PagePlus and PhotoPlus.

Peace and Healing For The World
Using Altars

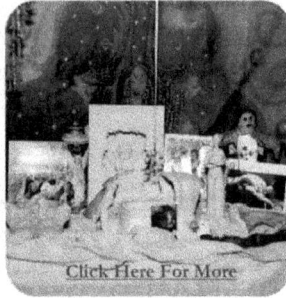

Written By
Lucretia and Gaila

The site below is for a book I wrote and my company, Positive Imaging, LLC, published.

Woodworking Business

Woodworking Business: Start Quickly And Operate Successfully

Woodworking skills are important to the success of a woodworking business but many other business skills are also required. After years in construction I started my woodworking business but it still took time to hone the skills needed to make the business profitable. Now I've decided to share the many proven techniques that were developed duing that time in my book "Woodworking Business: Start Quickly And Operate Successfully."

If you are already a competent woodworker wanting to start a woodworking business, or if you are already in the woodworking business but would like to increase your profit and simplify your work, **Woodworking Business: Start Quickly And Operate Successfully** is for you.

I started in construction at a young age but always enjoyed building cabinets. After leaving construction I spent over twenty years building cabinets and furniture for hundreds of customers. In spite of making many business mistakes while getting started I succeeded in the business. Now I have compiled all those years of lessons into my book **"Woodworking Business: Start Quickly And Operate Successfully."** It covers every step of how you can use your woodworking skills to make money.

Notice that all of the web sites are clean looking and easy to read and easy to create. In making the web sites the design of the book cover was considered. In most cases a small book cover photo, either flat or with a 3D appearance can be used. However, with some books, like the We Are All One book, the title and subtitle information is too small to read in a small size.

If go back and check the screen shot of that web site you'll see that the cover of the book is quite large and is integrated into overall design of the page. This makes it much easier to read the title and subtitle of the book.

On the Peace and Healing book on the left hand page, the cover is quite busy with the title, subtitle and several small pictures of individuals. For this site there is an introduction or lead in page that allows for the name of the book in large letters and large pictures of two of the altars pictured inside the book.

These are decisions that you will need to make if you wish to create your own web sites for your book or books.

If you aren't sure about creating a design you can hire a graphic artist to help you with a drawing or two and design the web site around them. Most often you can start your web site design by making the book cover an integral part or perhaps even use parts of the cover.

It's not really necessary to put a lot of graphics into a web site to market your book. What is necessary is to make it easy to find and purchase your book. In the page to the left showing the web site for the Woodworking Business book you can see the simplicity. It does have a picture of the book but the rest is writing in various sizes in text boxes that add emphasis to certain messages.

Throughout the text the idea is for the information to be down-to-earth and obviously an honest description of the benefits of the book. The entire thrust of the web site should be to put across how the potential purchaser would benefit from buying your book.

While you should mention a little about yourself, it should only be enough to show that you are highly competent to speak on the subject of the book. Remember, the web site is not about you. It is about what is in it for the potential buyer.

Before writing the content of your web site, list the keywords that apply to your book. As was previously indicated, the title of your book should be developed based on the best possible key words and then those same keywords are used on your web site. Good keywords will encourage the search engines to place your site high in rankings and this will help book sales.

The name of the book advertised on the web site about the Woodworking Business is followed by the subtitle. The title is an excellent keyword and because it is, the book remains high in search results and most importantly it was number one in Amazon.com searches for "woodworking business."

Books › "woodworking business"

Showing 1 - 12 of 1,613 Results   Sort by Relevance

Format

| Paperback | Hardcover | Kindle Edition | HTML | See more ˅ |
| (268) | (34) | (3) | (1,164) | |

LOOK INSIDE!

Woodworking Business: Start Quickly and Operate Successfully: An Expert Woodworker Reveals The Keys To Succeeding In The Woodworking Business by A. William Benitez (Apr 22, 2010)

☆☆☆☆☆ (2 customer reviews)

Formats	Price	New	Used
Paperback			
Order in the next 22 hours to get it by Wednesday, Dec 7 Eligible for FREE Super Saver Shipping	**$19.95**	$15.93	$17.83

Excerpt - Page 1: " even have your own small woodworking business and simply want to .." See a random page in this book.

Sell this back for an Amazon.com Gift Card

LOOK INSIDE!

The Woodworker's Guide to Pricing Your Work (Popular Woodworking) by Dan Ramsey (Apr 1, 2005)

☆☆☆☆☆ (6 customer reviews)

Formats	Price	New	Used
Paperback		$12.00	$5.44

This is what appeared when searching for "woodworking business" in the books category at Amazon.com. Notice that there are sixteen hundred results in this category so a mistake in selecting your title and your keywords can place your book completely out of sight and reduce sales. If sales are important to you, this has to be a major consideration because, at last report, Amazon sells sixty five percent of the books in the world. It's not a market to be ignored and neither is the importance of the search process.

The title of this woodworking business book is considered quite long and it is. However, it does convey exactly what you will find in the book before you ever turn the first page. If this is the kind of information you are looking for, the title quickly lets you know this is the place to look.

Just in case you have some doubts, the look inside feature provided by Amazon lets the prospective buyer open the book and check out important parts to make absolutely certain he or she will get the information for which they are searching.

At this point the potential buyer can either look inside the book or simply click on the link to go to the main sales page for the book. The screen shot on the next page illustrates the main sales page on Amazon.com. At this page you want to make certain that there are additional details about the book or even a review that includes some details.

This is also a good location for some information about the author of the book to indicate knowledge of the topic.

Using Web Sites & Blogs for Free Content

Obviously you want to sell copies of your book and marketing activities are essential but don't lose sight of various ways to use web sites and blogs to get prospective buyers interested in your book or books.

Free content is a great tool to draw interested prospects. The main objective of such content is to establish your expertise in whatever your niche happens to be. Below is a woodworking based web site that has been online for several years and is consistently on the first page of Google when searches are made.

I created this web site over eight years ago and it always has good traffic because it is on the first page of Google for "woodworking business" together with the sales page for my woodworking business book.

You can see that this web site has quite a bit on the first page. In addition to linking directly to many interesting articles on the woodworking business, it has an ad for the woodworking business book on the right side. That link takes you directly to the Woodworking Business sales web site.

Also, in the center of the page is a small box with information about a free course called Woodworking Simplified. This ecourse is distributed free by an autoresponder company that keeps track of information on anyone requesting the free ecourse. When someone fills in their first name and email address. The autoresponder sends out the ecourse in daily increments for a total of eight to ten days.

While autoresponders are good tools for email marketing, there are other good methods. Another method that also involves free content is to give away a complete ecourse on your web site. You can also work out arrangements with other writers or publishers to give away your ecourse as a bonus to their readers.

This free ecourse would have good solid content of value to the readers but also include links to your book's web site. With this method you shouldn't even ask for a name or email address. Make it a totally open, downloadable link and just count on the links within the course itself for potential customers to contact you. People are often more responsive to links that do not require any input.

At the top of the next page is a small ad for a free Handyman Business eBook or eCourse. A brief course was created for this give away for those who are interested in starting their own handyman business.

The free content is a 23 page eBooklet that is a summary of the book **The Handyman's Guide to Profit** which is a popular seller for Positive Imaging.

The eBooklet contains lots of information of real value to anyone interested in profiting from the handyman business and several links directly to the sales site for the handyman book.

FREE HANDYMAN BUSINESS EBOOK

Another FREE ebook? Sure, they are free except for name, email address, etc. and you wind up bombarded indefinitely. Not this time! This ebook is really FREE eCourse on how to start and operate a financially successful handyman business. Click the link, the ebook opens, you read it or save it to your PC and share it with friends. No name, no email, no obligation. Plus, got questions about the handyman business, just email bill@positive-imaging.com for free answers.

Click HERE for eCourse NOW.

A booklet like this can be most helpful with the marketing of non-fiction and how-to books but I believe there must be some way of taking advantage of such a booklet even for a fiction book. The important thing is that the booklet have real value and not simply be a sales pitch for your book.

There are many ways to create these booklets and the simplest one is to use a pdf file. Just create the booklet in any word processor or using PagePlus X4 and then convert the finished product to a pdf file for distribution.

The most common ebooklets are made in normal letter size. You can improve on this by creating your book in a size that better fits a standard monitor screen. This will ensure that the reader can see each page in full on the computer screen and then just move to the next page without scrolling.

To make it even better, you can use a pdf editing program to create bookmarks and navigation buttons on your booklet making it quite professional looking.

Does all that sounds like a lot of work for no money? In fact, everything you do to establish yourself as an expert in your field is time and money well spent. Being an expert will help you sell more ebooks.

Blogs are another way to distribute content that exhibits your extensive knowledge of any topic and there are many ways to create them. If you have created a web site and have your own domain name and a hosting arrangement, you can easily host a blog using your own domain name.

To do this you simply follow the instructions in your hosting providers support page and create a sub-domain or a folder. For example, you previously saw the sales web site for the Woodworking Business book. I created a folder within that same domain and now have a woodworking business blog where woodworkers can read posts and comment on them and no additional hosting expense.

The blog address is: http://woodworking-business.com/woodworkbiz and the blog is shown below:

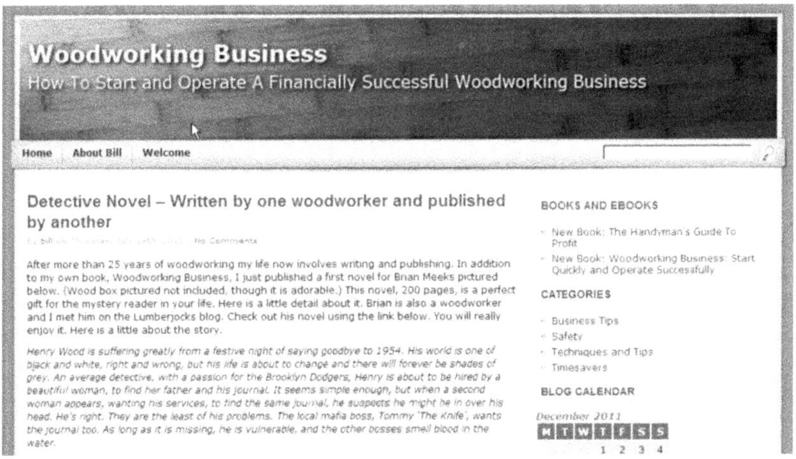

This blog has quite a lot of valuable information and links to free ebooklets. This particular post is about how one woodworker (me) had just published a book for another woodworker (Brian). The post is not really directly about woodworking or the woodworking business but it's still of interest to woodworkers.

Blogs can also be created directly in free blog sites like Wordpress, Blogspot, etc. I prefer to create blogs using the Wordpress software that's available within standard hosting programs.

For more information about web site hosting at the lowest prices and more details about creating your own web sites and blogs, email me at: bill@positive-imaging.com

Below is a screen shot of another blog on a different topics.

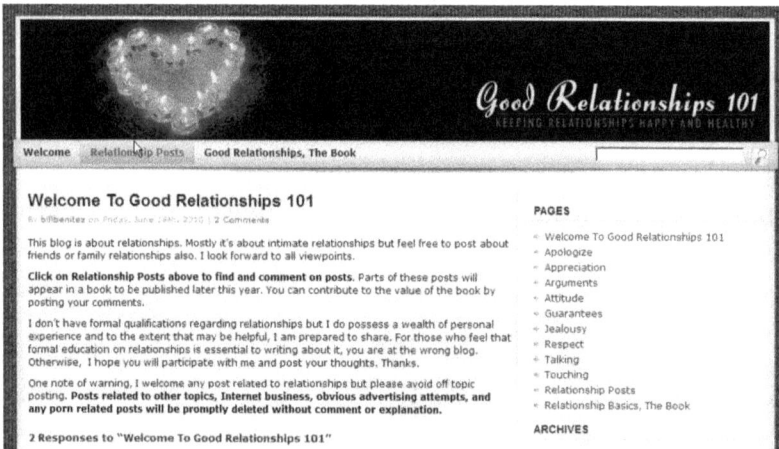

This blog is all about relationships and it also ties in with a book on the subject of happy and healthy relationships. I also have a web site for my relationship book which contains a complete press kit. You can check it out at http://notesonrelationship.com.

Below are more blog designs.

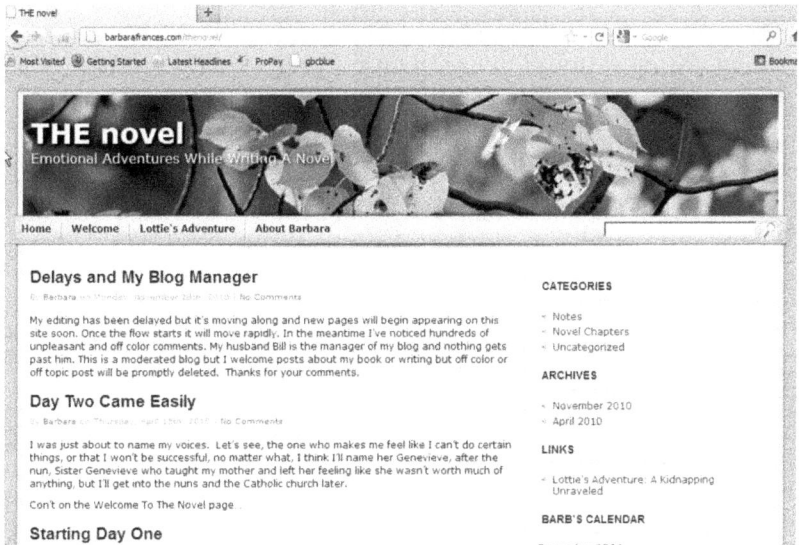

Notice the address on the blog above. This blog is set up as a sub-domain of the writer's web site. On the address of the blog below you can see that it is created on the Wordpress site. You can maintain a blog on this site absolutely free.

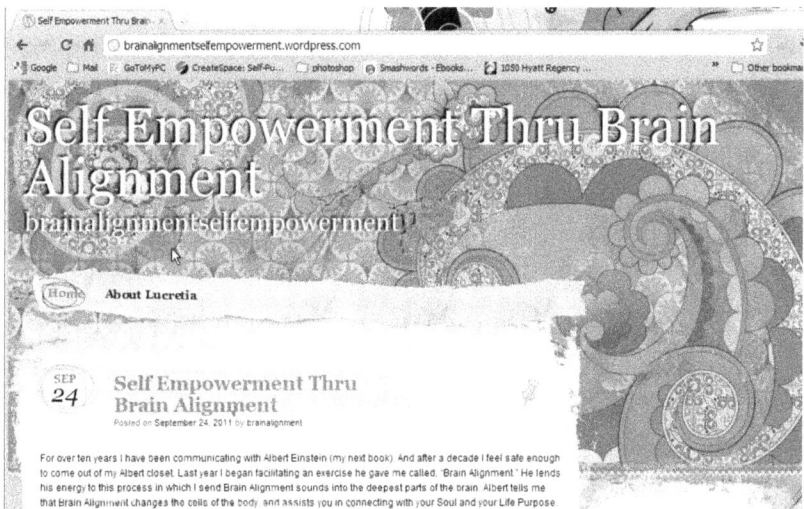

Creating free content does take time but I have definitely found it to be worth the effort. It clearly indicates that you value and want to serve your potential customers. Share your knowledge and you will encourage more purchases of your book.

Domain Names For Your Book Web Site

Some believe that getting a domain name should be the first step in creating a web site for a book or for content sharing. I prefer to create my web site and then use the content and design to lead me to a good domain name. Start by using your web site to develop good potential domain names. Don't just come up with one because it may be taken by someone else. You should have several options.

In creating potential domain names consider keywords that are related to your topic. Some topics are quite popular and you may find it difficult to get the domain name you choose. If that happens search for names that are close or for the same name with a descriptive word at the beginning or end. Strive to keep the important words in the domain name if possible.

Getting a good domain name for my previous book on self publishing is a prime example. I checked for the domain name selfpublishing and self-publishing and neither was available at the regular domain registration prices. But the domain registration site I use came up with quite a few options including the list on the next page.

All of those were available and I now own the last three on the list. I believe that the last one on the list will be best for the web site that I create for my book. I am considering buying one or two of the others.

Self-publishingtoday.com

Self-publishingshop.com

Self-publishingblog.com

Self-publishingnow.com

Self-publishingstore.com

Self-publishingsite.com

Qualityselfpublishing.com

Self-publishing-support.com

Publishingsimplified.com

Self-publish-your-writing.com

One way to get exactly the name you want is to use a sub-domain on a web site you already own. For example, I own the positive-imaging.com domain name. By going into my hosting management site I can create a sub-domain name selfpublishing or self-publishing and then the name of my book's web site could be:

selfpublishing.positive-imaging.com or

self-publishing.positive-imaging.com

This may work well for me because it contains the exact name of the book and it has the further advantage that I don't need to buy a domain name or web hosting since I am using an existing domain name and web site hosting account.

Web Site Hosting

There are many web site hosting companies that you can use to host your web sites. Go Daddy is one and Hostgator is another that I have dealt with for many years and they have always done a good job. They have all the services you could ever need at reasonable prices. You can buy your domain names and the hosting for your web site at a single location and they have excellent support services if you have questions or need assistance. There is no need to pay more for either domain names or for web hosting services. Go Daddy services are available at: http://godaddy.com .

There are other options and since I have more than 25 web sites and blogs, web hosting could have become quite costly. Instead of hosting my sites with a regular hosting arrangement, I became a web site hosting reseller for Hostgator. This allows me to host all my web site for only $24.95 per month plus I can sell web hosting services to others. Not only do my 25 plus web sites and blogs cost me less than $1.00 per month each to host, I make extra money selling web hosting services.

Hostgator offers an excellent service and support and makes maintaining your web sites quite easy. If your business involves many web sites it is definitely wise to consider a hosting reseller account with Hostgator. You can learn about it at http://hostgator.com .

Whether you choose Go Daddy, Hostgator, or some other domain registrar or web hosting company, most of them have excellent tutorials and tech services available for their customers. You can learn a great deal from them that will help you make better use of your web sites.

12

The Free Options

Creating a draft manuscript does not require an expensive word processor capable of handling complex office productivity. While it's not necessary to invest in Microsoft Office with MS Word if you don't already own it, I strongly recommend the investment. While Word has its flaws, I've found it to be an excellent tool over the years. There are options and I've listed some below.

Open Office

Open Office is a perfectly adequate office suite that is comparable to MS Office and capable of doing anything necessary to produce an outline and a draft manuscript. It is an easy download and install from the following website:

http://download.openoffice.org/

OpenOffice is open source software making it completely free and the website contains a great deal of valuable information and a community of users that participate actively.

In addition to being adequate for preparing manuscripts, it is an excellent office productivity suite that serves small businesses well. The learning curve for Open Office is similar to that of Microsoft Office but for creation of a manuscript, it is quite easy to use.

Scribus

The introduction to the Scribus application on their website states the following: "Scribus is an Open Source program that brings professional page layout to Linux/UNIX, Mac OS X, OS/2 Warp 4/eComStation and Windows desktops with a combination of press-ready output and new approaches to page design."

"Underneath a modern and user-friendly interface, Scribus supports professional publishing features, such as color separations, CMYK and Spot Color support, ICC color management, and versatile PDF creation."

Scribus has fascinated me for some time and I plan to learn to use it and begin with publishing a booklet to get a feel for it. I have played around with it and it seems to be great application with infinite potential and, most importantly, it is open source and therefore completely free. The application can be used for both formatting and layout but is also an excellent tool for creating book covers. As a good, all-in-one tool it merits the time to undergo its significant learning curve. I view that as a worthwhile effort and in time it may replace the Serif applications in my publishing business.

Scribus can be downloaded free at:

https://wiki.scribus.net/canvas/Download

Gimp

Gimp is an excellent application that is available free to anyone. It seems to be the equal of Photoshop, an excellent but expensive application from Adobe. On the Gimp website you will find the following details, "GIMP is the GNU Image Manipulation Program. It is a freely distributed piece of software for such tasks as photo retouching, image composition and image authoring. It works on many operating systems, in many languages."

"It has many capabilities. It can be used as a simple paint program, an expert-quality photo retouching program, an online batch processing system, a mass production image renderer, an image format converter, etc."

"GIMP is expandable and extensible. It is designed to be augmented with plug-ins and extensions to do just about anything. The advanced scripting interface allows everything from the simplest task to the most complex image-manipulation procedures to be easily scripted."

"GIMP is written and developed under X11 on UNIX platforms. But basically the same code also runs on MS Windows and Mac OS X."

> *Gimp has the advantages of Photoshop without the high price tag. I have used Gimp many times but am still in a learning phase. Since I own Photoshop and PhotoPlus X6, there isn't much motivation to learn a new graphics program. However, for those willing to meet the challenge of a lengthy learning curve, Gimp is the best deal around. It is another one of those applications I will get around to learn when time permits and I recommend it to anyone.*

Gimp can be downloaded free at: http://www.gimp.org/downloads/.

Photoscape

This is another good photo editing application. CNET editors gave it four stars and wrote the following about Photoscape: "Add another name to the roster of feature-rich freeware image editors: PhotoScape. Although it eats and leaks about as much memory as Firefox, this editor is perfect for those making the jump between JPEG and am-pro dSLR work."

"It supports RAW, as well as all other major image formats from JPEG and PNG to animated GIFs. It comes with prebuilt templates for users to create photo collages, fumetti, and Web comics, and has a standard set of red-eye removal, light/shadow, and contrast-editing features. One warning about the RAW processing: although it looks like you can drag and drop, the converter doesn't change RAW to JPEG unless you load the RAW file from within the native file navigator. It's a minor bug, but one that can lead you to believe that there's no RAW support at all. You can also batch edit images, combine them, and print them out one at a time or several at once."

> *In all honesty, I have only used Photoscape to process my vacation photos. I returned from Spain with over 1,300 digital photos and thought that I would face a nightmare editing, culling out, and preparing a slide show. Instead, Photoscape easily facilitated batch editing and made the job quite pleasant. So, if you need to edit a large number of photos, this is an excellent tool. It is also capable of much more in the hands of someone willing to learn how to use all of its features.*

Photoscape can be downloaded free at:

http://www.photoscape.org/ps/main/index.php

NVU

An excellent WYSIWYG website creation software. The publisher accurately describes it as: "Nvu (pronounced N-view, for a "new view") makes managing a web site a snap. Now anyone can create web pages and manage a web site with no technical expertise or knowledge of HTML. Finally! A complete Web Authoring System for Linux Desktop users as well as Microsoft Windows and Macintosh users."

> *I used NVU for years and still manage some of my websites with this easy to use application. Admittedly, I now use Serif's WebPlus for many of my websites because, like PagePlus and PhotoPlus, I find it easy to use and enjoy good support for the product. However,*

I highly recommend NVU as an excellent, free web creation application

Nvu can be downloaded free at:

http://download.cnet.com/Nvu/3000-10247_4-10412423.html

About Free Software Applications

If you spend any time on the web, you have received information about free software. It is readily available, and much of it is quite good. Unfortunately, many such applications come with hidden dangers including trojans (Viruses that hide inside tempting free software downloads.) that can damage your computer.

Since so much of this software is quite good, it is a good idea to make use of it to publish your ebook or to perform other computer-based tasks. There is a simple and safe way to make certain that the free software you download is safe and effective. You simply have to make certain that you only download software from safe locations on the web.

There are quite a few safe places to get free software but listed below are two that have been around for years and never include anything dangerous with the free software you download. These two are **CNET** and **SourceForge** and their main web sites are listed below.

http://www.cnet.com/ - this is the main site so just click the Download tab.
http://sourceforge.net/ - this is the main site where you just select your category and find free software.

Virus Protection Software

While on the subject of free software is a good time to deal with the issue of viruses. It's critical for those who work with computers, as do most writers and publishers, to protect their computers from viruses. This makes perfect sense but it's amazing how many people ignore the need for antivirus software or install the software and fail to update it on a regular basis. And, with the continued virus attacks across the Internet, updates are required almost every day.

Virus and spyware protection has become a growth industry, and there are many excellent tools on sale from reputable companies. One such reputable company that has proven itself over many years is Avast. In addition to their popular professional and reasonably priced Anti-virus and Internet security software, they have an excellent free product available for a simple registration.

Free Avast is available at the CNET website listed previously and at Avast.com. The CNET site states: "Avast made great strides in its previous update. Version 5 set the stage for the modern, massively popular, and free security suite with a new interface that ditched a quirky, late-'90s jukebox style for a more polished look. Easier to navigate, it also became easier to add new features."

"Make no mistake; Avast 6 adds features both big and small. Some that had previously only been available to paid upgrade users are now free for all versions, and newer features have been seamlessly added to the interface experience. If you're familiar with Avast 5, upgrading to Avast 6 won't be that big of a leap."

> I have used Avast for almost five years now on both my personal computer and my wife's and have always been well-protected. An excellent cost saving product.

Especially in a tough economy, it makes excellent sense to take full advantage of free quality software such as OpenOffice, Scribus, NVU, Gimp, and Avast. However, it is critical to search for safe products from safe locations to avoid having your computer contaminated by viruses.

What I Do As An Independent Publisher and Publishing Consultant

I help many authors to get their books published with consultation and coaching. In some cases, I handle the entire publishing process for authors while they maintain control of the process. If you need help to get published please visit my website at http://positive-imaging.com , email me at bill@positive-imaging.com , or call me at 512.217.4803. I'll be glad to discuss your ideas with no obligation.

If you want to publish a print book yourself but need some guidance, please check out my Self Publishing book. Complete information is available at my web site http://selfpublishingworkbook.com. Thank You!

After publishing a half dozen print books and several ebooks I began writing. **Self Publishing: How To Publish Your Print Book or eBook Step by Step**. It took a while to write because I wanted to cover every step of the methods I used in detail. This was the ninth book I published and have since published another dozen print books and over a dozen ebooks. It's not easy to publish a book alone, but it can be done and this book shows you how.

Here's what just a couple of experts have said about my book:

"At last, a clear an comprehensive guide through the self-publishing process, using free and/or inexpensive software."

Barbara Florio Graham, author and publishing consultant.

"This workbook is an amazing publishing guide for any author who wants to do it all him or herself."

Patricia Fry, author, speaker, editor

Excellent Self-Publishing Resource

If you are looking to publish your own books then **Self Publishing: How To Publish Your Print Book or eBook Step by Step** by A. William Benitez is a great resource for you. This book will help you to identify the steps you should take if you are looking to publish your own books. Benitez states that he identified these steps through many years of his own personal experience.

When you read **Self Publishing** you will learn the definition for the different types of publishing, including self-publishing. You will get help in planning your book from an idea through a full-fledged book including choosing great cover art, editing the content, and choosing the right formatting. In this book Benitez also will help you learn how to create a great searchable title as well as how to use both publishing software and productivity software. You'll also get Benitez's input on good point of delivery printers and ebook publishers.

This book is a great resource for all of your self-publishing needs.

Robin Perron

About A. William (Bill) Benitez

After spending much of my youth working in construction in Tampa, Florida, I went to work for local government managing federal assistance programs for several years and then as a consultant to government agencies. During those years I was asked to write a book about housing rehabilitation by the National Association of Housing and Redevelopment Officials, and it sold thousands of copies and while there was no payment I gained excellent national publicity. I parlayed that publicity into a one-person business writing, publishing, and consulting for local governments across the country. In addition to the consulting, I wrote and published seven more books and a monthly newsletter on housing rehabilitation.

This was well before the advent of POD so publishing those books involved a significant investment. After the presidential election of 1980, all the federal financing for housing rehabilitation activities dried up and the consulting and publishing business diminished. Finally, I returned to construction and home repair and then to the woodworking business I ran for over 20 years first in Tampa, Florida and then in Austin, Texas.

During those years in woodworking, I wrote and published a small book called "Simplified Woodworking I: A Business Guide For Woodworkers" and it sold well for a couple of years. I also published a newsletter called "Simplified Woodworking" that never really took off but was a good writing and publishing experience.

In 1998, in response to poor technical support for my wife's computer, I managed to fix it and that peaked my interest in computers. That early interest led me to move into information technology obtaining both an A+ and MCSE certification. For years I worked as both a computer technician and a network administrator for the Hyatt Regency Austin and retired from the position of IT Manager after twenty years.

In 2007 my wife wrote an excellent children's book but could not generate interest in it from a traditional publisher. Since I had published books years earlier, I decided to publish her book and began to learn all I could about POD. Publishing her book was a real learning experience and it took several tries to get my files approved for printing. After that I published a book that I wrote on the woodworking business and decided to start my publishing company. Since then my company Positive Imaging, LLC has published more than twenty four print books and over a dozen ebooks on Kindle, Smashwords, and Clickbank.

I enjoy sharing all kinds of information with others and spend a lot of time every day answering questions. I honestly believe that anyone willing to take the time to follow the steps described in this book can learn how to publish quality ebooks.

Disclaimer

Everything described in this book is based on my personal experience. Over the years, I have gained much experience in the publishing business and published over twenty four print books and over a dozen ebooks. I am a competent, though not extraordinary, businessperson. Anyone with good computer skills and a sincere desire to learn may be able to attain similar results if he or she puts in the effort. Nevertheless, no guarantees are expressed or implied regarding your results using the information in this book.

Some individuals are more apt to profit from independently publishing books and/or ebooks than others due to the level of their skills, business acumen, and communication abilities. Regardless of my experience over the years, I can't guarantee that you will succeed in this or any business.

Business of any kind involves the risk of loss, including, but not necessarily limited to, money, time, and energy. I have made every effort to accurately describe my experiences in detail but cannot be held liable for the success or failure of your independent publishing venture.

This book includes the names of and information about several brand name products. All of these are products I have personally used but I own no interest in any of the manufacturers or distributors of these products nor have I received any payment for listing them in this book. I list them solely because they have worked for me and they are reasonably priced or free.

The user of this information agrees that he or she is solely responsible for the consequences of using any products described in this book. It is also the user's responsibility to conduct a reasonable level of due diligence before making any business or legal decisions. The information contained and distributed in this book is not intended as nor should it be considered professional, business, or legal advice.

For any questions please contact

bill@positive-imaging.com

Notes

www.ingramcontent.com/pod-product-compliance
Lightning Source LLC
Chambersburg PA
CBHW070538030426
42337CB00016B/2256